MY ANCESTOR WAS A BASTARD

A FAMILY HISTORIAN'S GUIDE TO SOURCES FOR ILLEGITIMACY IN ENGLAND AND WALES

by Ruth Paley

D1344302

SOCIETY OF GENEALOGISTS ENTERPRISES LTD

Published by
Society of Genealogists Enterprises Limited
14 Charterhouse Buildings
Goswell Road
London EC1M 7BA

First Edition © Ruth Paley 2004
Reprinted 2007, 2008, 2009
Revised reprint 2011

ISBN: 978-1-903462-78-2

British Library Cataloguing in Publication Data
A CIP Catalogue record for this book is available from the British Library

About the Author
Ruth Paley is a legal historian. Despite the advice contained in this guide,
she has yet to trace the real parents of her grandfather who was baby
farmed long before the creation of formal adoption records.

Society of Genealogists Enterprises Limited is a wholly owned subsidiary of
Society of Genealogists, a registered charity, no 233701

Cover illustration
Foreground: Untitled photograph from the 'Baker-Holl' special collection at
Society of Genealogists. Background (document): Bastardy examination of
Mary Morris, January 1779, from the parish chest of All Saint's, Staplehurst,
deposited at the Centre for Kentish Studies in Maidstone. Reference P347/15/1

FOREWORD

The purpose of this book is not just to help family historians find the sources that will solve a particular problem, but also to help them to understand that problem by giving it a wider historical context. Family history is something more than hanging as many names as possible on a pedigree chart, it is also about studying the experiences, values and beliefs of our ancestors. This book was conceived (if you will pardon the expression) in an attempt to help you do both.

It was not until I had started writing that I realised just how difficult the task would be. I am grateful to all those who have come to my rescue by reading and commenting on earlier drafts; each has not only suggested useful improvements but has corrected my mistakes. Amanda Bevan, Paul Brand and John Titford have heroically read the entire text; Anne Cole helped with the section on pre-1834 poor law records, David Prior helped with records of divorce and David Annal and Kieron Mahoney checked the sections referring to the then Family Records Centre (now The National Archives or General Register Office as appropriate). All remaining errors are, of course, entirely my own responsibility.

Ruth Paley
May 2003

CONTENTS

PART III: FINDING & USING THE SOURCES

PART IV: FINDING YOUR WAY AROUND

LIST OF ILLUSTRATIONS

Sources:

Illustrations 2-9 courtesy of London Metropolitan Archives.

Section numbers:

Section numbers are indicated by references in square brackets within the text, e.g. [**31**]

PART I: ILLEGITIMACY IN CONTEXT

1. Introduction

Illegitimacy, like poverty, is always with us: most families have at least one if not several instances of it in their ancestry. But – surprisingly for a condition that is so pervasive – it is very difficult to define. At its most simplistic it is about children born to parents who are not married to each other. But what of children born to women who are married to someone other than the father? Or of polygamous unions? Or women who are single because their marriages have been ended by separation or death? What of children born to parents who were not married at the time of birth but who married later? What of parents who believe themselves to be married but whose unions turn out not to be legally valid? Or, to make it still more complicated, parents whose marriages are valid in one society but not in another?

None of these questions is easy to answer because illegitimacy is a concept that derives from a complex mixture of legal, religious, moral and cultural factors. That is why it has been (and for some people still is) an extremely emotive issue. Illegitimacy has always been defined as a problem and those deemed to be illegitimate have suffered stigmatisation, discrimination and legal disability. Even the words we use to describe it are emotionally charged. Just think of the range of meanings attached to the word 'bastard'. Technically, it means born out of wedlock but in practice, as we all know, it can be (and often is) used as a term of abuse rather than as a reflection on the marital status of an individual's parents. In the past bastardy resulted in a range of discriminatory behaviours. Some schools would not admit illegitimate children. Early maternity or 'lying in' hospitals refused their services to any but respectable married women. Bastards were barred as children from orphanages (meant for the care of the children of the respectable) and as adults from the professions and from holding military commissions or joining the priesthood. The illegitimate were perceived as having 'bad blood' and fictional bastards were commonly portrayed as archetypal villains, often, like Caliban in Shakespeare's *Tempest*, revealing their evil personalities by an outward physical deformity. When the evil Edmund in Shakespeare's *King Lear* commands the gods to 'Stand up for bastards' he is not asking for tolerance and understanding of human frailty but signalling disorder and misrule.

Unless you are very lucky indeed, tracing information about illegitimate ancestors will never be straightforward and it may in the end prove to be impossible. But by making an effort to understand something about the economic, cultural and legal boundaries that shaped the world of the unmarried mother and her child, then you will at least be able to make educated guesses about the searches that are most likely to get results. This guide is intended to help you do just that. However, you need to be aware that it is based overwhelmingly on English and Welsh sources. If your illegitimate ancestors were born in Scotland or Ireland, you will need to take additional specialist advice from someone who is more familiar with legal structures and record creation in those countries.

In the course of writing this guide it has become apparent that tracing illegitimate ancestors can be a problem for all family historians, however experienced or inexperienced they may be. It has therefore been written in the belief that at least some of its users will be total novices and that those researching nineteenth- and twentieth-century ancestors may need a higher level of advice and help than those who have successfully pursued their ancestors back into an earlier period.

This guide attempts to be comprehensive both in its discussion of sources and the social context of illegitimacy from approximately 1300 to 1950. Changes in attitudes to illegitimacy and marriage before and after that date are outside its scope. It also assumes that children were conceived by natural means: it does not address problems that are specific to the years since 1950, such as the difficulties of tracing parentage for children conceived as a result of artificial insemination by donor, or of donor reproductive material used in *in vitro* fertilisation.

This guide is arranged in four parts. Part I provides an introduction to the social history of illegitimacy, but please remember that it *is* only a introduction: bastardy is a complex subject and that if you want to investigate it in more depth you will need to read more widely. The books listed in section 16 will help you to broaden your focus. Part II concentrates on how to formulate a search strategy, giving a few tips and pointing out some of the more common pitfalls that researchers can fall into. Part III describes some of the sources and their locations in more detail. Part IV contains practical information designed to make finding and using the sources as easy as possible. Each section of the guide is numbered and to save space and repetition, the section numbers (highlighted in bold) are used for cross-references: so that [23] is an indication that you would find it useful to look at section 23 which deals with adoption records.

2. Illegitimacy and inheritance

The definitions and consequences of illegitimacy vary not only over time but also from community to community, even within a geographical area as small as the British Isles. Strange though it may seem, it was possible for a child to be legitimate in one of the three kingdoms (England and Wales; Scotland; Ireland) of the British Isles but not in one or both of the others. In the mid 1760s, for example, Arthur Annesley, a young aristocrat, who was attempting to claim his father's peerage, was somewhat bizarrely 'proved' to be legitimate in Ireland but illegitimate in England. Half a century later, the succession to the Scottish earldom of Strathmore rested entirely on deciding whether Scots or English law should decide the legitimacy of a child born in England to Scots parents.

The legal system in England and Wales was quite different to that of the rest of Europe. English and Welsh law, known as common law, derived from the established customs of the realm. The common law was also used in Ireland. Although the English and Irish used the same system of law, the courts of the two countries were separate and could therefore reach different conclusions about the same evidence. This is what happened in the Annesley case. The question was not whether Arthur Annesley's parents were married but *when* they married. Under the common law a child could not be legitimated by the subsequent marriage of its parents. Arthur Annesley was legitimate if his parents married before his birth; if (as stated by a rival claimant) they married *after* his birth, then he was illegitimate. The Irish House of Lords chose to believe that his parents married before he was born; the English House of Lords did not. As a result, Arthur Annesley inherited his father's Irish peerage, but not his English one.

The peculiarities of the Annesley decision stem from differences in applying the law. In the Strathmore case, the situation was complicated by much more fundamental differences in the law itself. In Scotland (and all other European countries) the legal system is based on Roman rather than common law. Under Roman law, the child of an unmarried couple is legitimated by the subsequent marriage of its parents, *provided they were free to marry at the time of its birth.* No one denied that John Bowes, infant son of the bachelor Earl of Strathmore, was illegitimate at birth, but as the Earl lay dying, he tried to put things right. He was carried to church where he married John's mother, just one day before his death. Since the Earl was a Scotsman, holding Scottish lands and Scottish titles, he was convinced that Scots law would apply to the legitimacy of his son, and he knew that under Scots law his marriage rendered the child unquestionably legitimate. But the Earl lived in London; he was married in London and his son was born in London. Under English law the child was unquestionably illegitimate. The House of Lords decided English law should prevail and the son was barred from inheriting his father's titles.

These two cases illustrate what to most lay people appear to be the absurdities of the legal system. They also illustrate the importance of the connection between legitimacy and inheritance. Illegitimacy was not simply about social disabilities; it was very much about legal rights (or rather the lack of them). Early medieval law did not distinguish easily between legitimate and illegitimate children but by about the thirteenth century, the status of an illegitimate child was very different to that of a legitimate one. The common law deemed a bastard to be *filius nullius* which means 'no one's child' or *filius populi* 'child of the people'. In other words, it had no legal relatives. It had no right to carry the surname(s) of its birth parents, still less to be regarded as their next of kin. Until the early twentieth century (with one exception), an illegitimate child could not inherit anything (even from its mother) unless specific legal arrangements were made to ensure the transmission of wealth. This could be done by making a settlement (a legal device designed to get round the inheritance laws) or by making a bequest in a will. However, a will that favoured a bastard over a legitimate child was open to challenge and likely to be overturned by the courts. The one exception to the normal inheritance rules was that of medieval villeinage: a child born to a villein mother followed her status whether legitimate or illegitimate. If an illegitimate person died unmarried and intestate, his or her estate would be forfeit (if held under feudal tenure in early times) to the feudal lord or (since medieval times) to the crown (but see **44**). No illegitimate child could inherit a title, so he was automatically deprived of the social status of the rest of his family. In a highly stratified and status conscious society like Britain, this was a very real deprivation. Charles II was in a better position than most to provide for his bastards. He is famous for conferring lands and dukedoms on his children: but to be a Duke, however wealthy, was scarcely the same as being a prince with an acknowledged right to inherit the crown. The Duke of Monmouth was Charles II's eldest son, but his attempts to be proclaimed as his heir led him to the scaffold instead of to the throne.

There were some compensations for the lack of legal status. Under statute and common law, the proposition that an illegitimate child had no legal parents led to the corollary that (s)he could not be compelled to support them if they fell on hard times and needed poor relief. This had not been the case in medieval times when church law was more widely used [**10**]. Nor did the illegitimate have to seek parental consent to marry under the age of 21. It is difficult to argue however that the advantages could often (ever?) have outweighed the disadvantages.

3. Legal definitions of illegitimacy

Under the common law, a child was legitimate if:
- it was conceived and born in a valid marriage; or
- it was conceived before marriage but its parents entered into a valid marriage before it was born; or
- it was conceived during a valid marriage but born after the marriage had been ended.

Equally the child was not legitimate if:
- the parents' marriage was not valid; or
- if the father could be proved to be someone other than the mother's husband

A child conceived in one marriage but born during a subsequent marriage was deemed to be the legitimate offspring of the earlier marriage. Until the fifteenth century, if the parents' marriage was not valid but they did not know of the impediment, the child remained legitimate even if the marriage were dissolved.

The common law presumed that the husband of a woman who bore a child was the father of that child, even if the marriage took place after conception. This presumption could be challenged, usually by proof of no intercourse, but the disabilities that attached to illegitimacy were so great that, until the mid twentieth century, the courts required the husband to prove his case beyond all possible doubt. This was extremely difficult. Blood tests, which until the advent of DNA testing, were the only scientific means of eliminating some (but not all) paternal suspects, were not available until the twentieth century and even then were not compulsory. Proof of separation did not amount to proof of no intercourse unless one of the parties was actually abroad at the time of conception.

Repudiation by the husband was a necessary pre-condition of declaring the child of a married woman to be illegitimate, but it was not enough in itself to bastardise it. An interesting example of this occurred in the Ampthill peerage case. In 1921, Lord Ampthill attempted to divorce his wife on the grounds of adultery committed by her with some unknown person. The evidence adduced was simple enough: Lord Ampthill's marriage had never been consummated, yet his wife had produced a baby boy. Lady Ampthill, for her part, did not dispute that she had never had full intercourse with her husband. In fact she produced medical evidence to prove that she had never had full intercourse with anyone. According to her, the child had been conceived during a failed attempt at marital rape. Lord Ampthill never accepted that the child was his, but such a belief – no matter how sincerely held – was not enough to persuade the courts to refuse a declaration of legitimacy or, after his death, to convince the House of Lords to withhold the peerage from the disputed son.

Even a declaration by both parents that the child was fathered by someone other than the husband was insufficient to bastardise it, since it was argued that the parents might collude to force another person to raise their child. The only recourse open to a husband who believed that his wife had foisted her lover's child upon him was to seek a private Act of Parliament to bastardise the child(ren). Where a marriage had broken down this far, it was likely that the husband would also be seeking a divorce, and it became standard practice to insert a bastardisation clause into divorce bills [32].

As indicated earlier, the common law did not allow for legitimisation by a subsequent marriage. This remained true until 1926 when Parliament brought English law in line with Scots law, legitimising children born before their parents' marriage as long as they were free to marry at the time of the birth. Since 1959 English law has permitted a child to be legitimised by the subsequent marriage of its parents, even if they were *not* free to marry at the time of its birth. It has also been possible, since 1858, for an individual to petition for a decree of legitimacy, which is binding against all future legal actions. Before that date individuals could obtain much the same result by obtaining a ruling in the course of a legal action that was ostensibly brought for another purpose; such actions were often collusive. Legitimisation of a child by the subsequent marriage of its parents does not confer inheritance rights for all kinds of property: entailed estates and titles still descend by the old common law rules.

There were other systems of justice in use alongside the common law courts in England and Wales. Many disputes over property were settled in courts that applied rules of 'equity' [31] but which used common law rules about legitimacy. The church also had courts of its own. Since church law (sometimes known as canon or ecclesiastical law), like Scots law, was based on Roman law, it defined illegitimacy in the same way. So, just to confuse things still further, it was possible for the same individual to be regarded as legitimate by one set of English courts and illegitimate by another.

4. Courtship and marriage

In the western world we now take efficient contraception for granted. Nor, by and large, do we have any moral qualms about using it. Matters were very different for our ancestors. Some birth control measures, such as *coitus interruptus* and the rhythm method, were known and used, but they were not particularly reliable. Condoms were also used, though more to protect against venereal disease than as contraceptives. Birth control was widely believed to be immoral and provoked fierce public debate well into the middle of the twentieth century. For the purposes of this guide, therefore, it is assumed that pregnancy was the almost inevitable consequence of sexual intercourse.

The effects of malnourishment apart, it seems unlikely that the human sex drive has changed over the centuries. However, it is clear that the social and moral context within which couples enter into sexual relationships has varied markedly. Societies with strong social controls against pre-marital sex have lower illegitimacy rates than those that do not. In the mid seventeenth century, at the height of the puritan ascendancy over everyday life and morality, the rate in England and Wales was less than 2%. There was a marked rise in the later eighteenth century and in 1860, at the height of what we usually regard as repressive Victorian attitudes, it was 6.5%. Social attitudes may then have become *more* rather than less repressive because the rate slowly declined until in the first half of the twentieth century (apart from bulges in the war years) it had settled at a fairly steady 4%.

Available statistical evidence suggests that the illegitimacy rate in Ireland has always been lower (even in the nineteenth century it never reached 4%). Illegitimacy rates of Irish communities in England however were very much higher, and were the subject of much comment at the time of the 1834 Poor Law Amendment Act. This was at least partly because the law was very different in the two countries: Hardwicke's Marriage Act [5] meant that marriages celebrated in English Roman Catholic churches were not legally valid, most children born to Irish Catholic couples in England were therefore technically illegitimate, even if their parents considered themselves to be married in the sight of God. To the chagrin of those (mainly Scots) contemporaries who believed Calvinism fostered higher moral standards than Roman Catholicism, the illegitimacy rate in nineteenth-century Scotland was the highest in the British Isles. It ran at around 9% in the mid nineteenth century and then dropped steadily, evening out at a little under 6% in the first half of the twentieth century (again with bulges in the war years).

Statistical surveys of this kind are useful but they need to be treated with care, especially when they disguise marked local or regional patterns. In 1946 the illegitimacy rate in England and Wales stood at what was then a twentieth-century high: 6.6%. This disguised variations from less than 5% (Brecknock and Cumberland) to over 11% (Anglesey and the Soke of Peterborough). Similar regional variations occurred in Scotland and Ireland. Some of the variations are difficult to explain. Why should illegitimacy be higher in Suffolk than in neighbouring Essex? Why in 1907 was the illegitimacy rate 18% in Marylebone but only 1.5% just a few miles away in Stepney, Mile End and Bethnal Green? There are even regional patterns to marriages *after* the birth of an illegitimate child. One study found that between 1550 and 1650 90% of single mothers in the southeast and eastern midlands married the fathers of their children within a year of birth but that it took five years to achieve the same result in the northwest.

Although nearly 7% of children born in mid nineteenth century England were illegitimate, about 20%-30% of nineteenth-century brides were pregnant when they married. In 1945, 40% of babies born had been conceived before their parents were married. In one Cumberland parish (Lamplugh) during the first two decades of the seventeenth century an astonishing 60% of brides were pregnant. These simple statistics illustrate a basic point: counting illegitimate births is not necessarily a good guide either to levels of pre-marital sexual activity or to the prevailing moral attitudes that shape the context in which it takes place.

In the early modern period, correlating dates of marriage to dates of birth demonstrates that in some areas most pregnant brides were in early pregnancy, suggesting that the decision to commence a sexual relationship followed the decision to marry. Elsewhere, brides were more likely to be at an advanced stage of pregnancy, suggesting that the decision to marry followed the pregnancy. A study of illegitimacy in the Second World War shows that although the illegitimacy rate rose, there was a similar fall in pre-marital conceptions. Put another way, there were more illegitimate children but fewer 'shotgun' marriages. This kind of analysis enables us to see that the cultural context of courtship differed from community to community and from age to age. Nor should we forget that at all periods certain sub-groups held very different attitudes to those of their mainstream community. The last quarter of the twentieth century saw major changes in social attitudes and family structures. Most readers of this book will find it difficult to understand a society in which shame can be felt so deeply that members of a family would conspire together to kill a woman in the seventh month of pregnancy because she was pregnant by someone other than her husband. Yet that is precisely what happened in 1998 to a nineteen-year-old in Derbyshire whose family originated from the Indian sub-continent.

Detailed analysis of bastardy and bridal pregnancy in the past is often difficult because the quality of information available to us is so poor. Until 1837 we do not have information about births but about *baptisms* and we know that bastards were less likely to be baptised than legitimate children. Nationally, the very low illegitimacy rate in the mid seventeenth century could mean that the prevailing puritan ethic actually reduced extra-marital sexual activity. It could also mean that more pregnant girls rushed into marriage or that a higher proportion of bastards was not baptised at all, or it could be a combination of all these factors. It is also true that a disproportionate number of illegitimate children died as very young babies and went unbaptised for that very reason.

Even after civil registration was introduced in 1837, there are many distortions and inaccuracies in the statistics. Extrapolations from infant mortality statistics suggest that illegitimate babies were more likely to be stillborn, but stillbirths were not registered until 1926. In practice many children went unregistered: although registration was compulsory, there was no penalty for failure to register until 1875. In modern Britain documentary proof of age and/or birthplace is essential for almost all aspects of everyday life: getting jobs, bank accounts, mortgages, passports, social security, insurance, pensions. Life was very different for our ancestors. Most people rented rather than bought their homes. Very few ever travelled abroad, and even if they did, they would not need a passport (passports became common only after the First World War). Why bother to register a child if you were never going to need the certificate – and perhaps were not even able to read it? Registration levels probably improved as the century wore on, but as late as 1874, a third of all births in Liverpool went unregistered, and the same was probably true of many other areas. If under-registration was a problem for legitimate births, it was almost certainly a far greater problem for illegitimate ones.

Although it is impossible to quantify levels of pre-marital sex, it is clear that in some communities pre-marital sex was perfectly acceptable. Until 1754 betrothal (often called the 'spousals') could have two meanings. It could of itself create a legal marriage, or it could simply be a promise to marry with a corresponding agreement to make appropriate property arrangements. An agreement to marry might be considered sufficient to mark the beginning of an acceptable sexual relationship. Acceptable, that is, to the couple's immediate community. The church regarded such matters rather differently. Furthermore, its condemnation of adultery, fornication and pre-marital conception was backed by the church courts – often known, not surprisingly, as the 'bawdy courts'. These courts relied on the power of shame rather than fines or imprisonment: a typical punishment would require individuals to perform penance by standing in church during Sunday service covered in a white sheet. You can find an excellent taster of the kind of cases they dealt with and the punishments they inflicted from the 'Penance' website at Leicester University [46]. In the worst cases church courts could order excommunication, which in the medieval period could of itself result in imprisonment. The church courts fell into disuse during the English Civil War and Commonwealth of the mid-seventeenth century, but were re-established in 1660. Their comeback soon lost momentum and by the end of the seventeenth century their authority was in major decline – although there were certainly some areas of the country where the church court is known to have continued imposing penalties well into the eighteenth century.

In the seventeenth and early eighteenth centuries such offences were also prosecuted at courts of quarter sessions. In some areas almost every case of bastardy resulted in a prosecution in the church courts. In others only about 50% of them. In some areas laxity on the part of the church courts was complemented by zealous prosecutions at quarter sessions; in others it was not. Some individuals found themselves prosecuted, and punished, by both courts. The pattern of activity both over time and from one geographical area to another is so inconsistent that you may find it necessary to search several sets of records [30]. In medieval times, fornication and bastard bearing were also punishable by the manorial courts, who could impose penalties ranging from whipping to fines known as leyrwite (sometimes legerwite) and childwite on the unfree. Depending on the custom of the manor, bastardy could have far-reaching consequences for both mother and child. Being deemed a bastard could bar a manorial tenant from inheritance; becoming a bastard bearer could lead to the loss of lands, as Dulcia Telat of Cranfield in Bedfordshire discovered to her cost in 1312 [36]. You can read about her case in the volume by Poos and Bonfield [45].

In some parts of early modern Britain (and parts of Europe and New England), serious courtship in the lower classes was said to have been associated with 'bundling'. This involved the couple quite literally spending the night together. Activities associated with bundling ranged from the conversational to a variety of sexual activities that were supposed to fall well short of full intercourse. In other areas, including the Isle of Portland, full-scale trial marriages were common: the couple being expected to marry as and when they wished to do so or if a pregnancy ensued, but also being free to separate and form new relationships without stigma.

Higher up the social scale matters were necessarily rather different. From the royal family to comparatively humble yeomen farmers, marriage was a matter of business: securing both the consolidation of property and its transmission to the next generation. The pressure to marry well for dynastic/financial reasons could be intense. Arranged marriages in which neither party had much of a say, or in extreme cases may not have actually met, were common in the medieval and even in the early modern period. The rise of ideas associating marriage with companionship and love introduced more choice and independence for the young people concerned, but one suspects that the lower-class couple who had bundled together through the night were rather more likely to have explored a companionable relationship than their closely chaperoned social superiors. Relationships between the sexes in the upper classes (and increasingly in the middling ranks of society too) were very formalised. For some – perhaps most – this very formality provided a certain level of security in that it defined expectations and patterns of acceptable behaviour between the sexes. For others it clearly had quite the opposite effect: young women were unable to act naturally for fear of compromising their reputations; young men were equally frightened of discovering that they had unwittingly become suitors instead of friends (or even mere acquaintances).

Books and pamphlets on how to conduct oneself in a socially acceptable way (often known as 'courtesy books') were very popular in the eighteenth and nineteenth centuries, for this very reason. Similar themes also turn up in popular novels and plays. The plot of Oliver Goldsmith's play, *She Stoops to Conquer* (first performed in 1773), struck a chord with its audiences precisely because the young hero's problem – his inability to enter into any kind of relationship with a woman who is his social equal – was uncomfortably close to reality. Many upper-class men felt safer with a mistress than with a wife. Some, like Sir Richard Ford who fathered several children by his mistress, the actress Dorothea Jordan, went on to make respectable marriages with more 'suitable' partners (she also moved onwards and upwards; her next lover was a royal duke). Occasionally they threw caution to the winds and married their mistresses – sometimes, like the 5th Earl Berkeley, so secretly that polite society was left uncertain as to whether a marriage had or had not taken place, and which of the various children of the relationship were and were not legitimate. The Earl went to considerable lengths to ensure that the eldest son of his long relationship with Mary Cole (reputedly the daughter of a butcher and most definitely not a suitable match for an eighteenth century aristocrat) would inherit his title. He even attempted to forge a marriage entry in the parish register. He failed, and after his death the eldest son was declared to be illegitimate.

Matters were, of course, rather different for those deemed to be the 'weaker' sex. For some girls mere loss of reputation – let alone actual pregnancy – could sometimes be enough to hasten a marriage. This in itself might provide a motive for seduction by an unscrupulous male in search of a fortune, modest financial security or (like Joe Lampton in John Braine's 1957 novel, *Room at the Top*) enhanced career prospects. Those abandoned without marriage might consider the option of suing for damages. The girl herself could bring an action for breach of promise or her parent (usually her father, but occasionally a widowed mother) could bring an action for compensation for loss of the daughter's services [31].

Such an action could lead to substantial damages and effectively provide the girl with a dowry big enough to restore her marriageability, but it was a risky business. This sort of action was expensive; the size of the damages was likely to be proportionate to the girl's previous respectability and social status, and no parent was going to be able to claim for loss of services if the daughter had already left home. In other words, rich, well-connected girls who did not have to work for a living were going to get higher damages than poor ones, and a live-in domestic servant was unlikely to get anything at all. A legal action was also almost certainly going to attract unwelcome publicity.

Although we know that many upper-class women embarked on affairs *after* marriage, and that the paternity of some of their children was a matter of speculation and sometimes of common knowledge, pregnancies that resulted in illegitimate children *before* marriage are difficult to find. Even when we suspect their existence, they are difficult to confirm. The antiquary and local historian William Robinson was illegitimate. Unlike most illegitimate children, it is not his paternity but his maternity that is in doubt. He was brought up by his father, also named William Robinson, and never knew his mother. Family folklore identified her as Ann Nelson, sister of Horatio. Ann Nelson died unmarried at a young age; there is no indication in the story of the Nelson family that she had ever had a relationship with an unsuitable young man, that she became pregnant, how and why she was persuaded not to marry the father or to give him their child. The Nelsons were well connected but they were far from being rich or aristocratic; if they could conceal the existence of the child so successfully, how much easier would it have been for the truly wealthy?

5. Marriage

In medieval times, legally-binding marriages could be undertaken in a variety of ways. Public marriage in a church, after the calling of banns, created a legal marriage. Clergymen also conducted marriages in a variety of other premises, of which perhaps the most notorious was the Fleet prison in London. Couples could also be married by declaration. There were two kinds of declaration:

- *verba de praesenti* – a declaration in the present tense by each of the couple that they were marrying each other.
- *verba de futuro* – a declaration by the couple that they intended to marry in the future, sometimes called the spousals. The marriage became legally binding on consummation.

In some parts of the country, these declarations were sometimes accompanied by simple ceremonies such as joining of hands or jumping over a broomstick together. A 'broomstick marriage' was slang for cohabitation well into the nineteenth century. Indeed, as we enter the twenty-first century this ancient custom is being revived by both African-Americans and neo-pagans as part of a conscious reinvention of traditional pre-Christian rites.

Marriages which were not celebrated in church, even if performed by a clergyman, or which resulted from cohabitation and declaration, were frowned upon by the church. Participating clergy were liable to disciplinary measures in the church courts, as were the couples themselves. Nevertheless they did create a legal and binding marriage, although under the common law children would not be regarded as legitimate and the wife would not become entitled to dower unless the marriage were public. Almost by definition, however, such marriages were unlikely to be recorded anywhere. Not surprisingly, it was sometimes difficult to be sure that people really were legally married or to prevent them from bigamous unions. It was also very easy for young or inexperienced people to find themselves unintentionally married, or to be tricked into marriage. Neither church nor common law prohibited marriage between children – defined as girls under 12 and boys under 14 – but such marriages could be voided unless the children concerned cohabited once those ages were reached.

In 1753 the passing of Hardwicke's Marriage Act introduced major reforms. The Act required couples intending to marry to do so in the parish church or other public chapel after the calling of banns (public notice of their intention to marry) on three successive Sundays. Those under 21 required the consent of their parents/guardians, although the age of marriage remained unchanged (still 14 for a boy and 12 for a girl). It was not until 1929 that the age of marriage was set at 16 for both sexes. The marriage had to be conducted by an ordained minister of the Church of England: the only exceptions allowed (until 1837) were for Jewish and Quaker ceremonies. Couples wishing to avoid the calling of banns could do so by obtaining a licence from the bishop or archbishop or other senior ecclesiastical officer, but this was very much more expensive. The public registration of the marriage also became compulsory. Clergymen who conducted weddings in contravention of the Act were punished severely (conviction could lead to a sentence of transportation for 14 years). The Act did not apply to Scotland where marriages by declaration continued to be legal and to be legally recognised in England and Wales: hence the notoriety of elopement to marriage shops in Gretna Green and other towns just across the Scottish border.

Hardwicke's Marriage Act was controversial. Some people thought it gave parents (especially rich, aristocratic ones) too much control over their children's choice of partner. In a century when it had become increasingly fashionable for the upper classes to marry by licence, some argued that the calling of banns was indecent since it amounted to a public declaration that the couple concerned would be having sex on a particular night. Many people thought that the government had no right to interfere in matters that more properly concerned the church: in 1758, Thomas Turner recorded in his diary that two clergymen were imprisoned unjustly in Horsham Gaol 'For acting contrary to the laws of men, but not, in my opinion, to the laws of GOD – that is, for marrying contrary to the Marriage Act'. Turner's diary is widely available since it was published as *The diary of a Georgian shopkeeper* by Oxford University Press in 1979. Some people ignored the provisions of the Act and continued to marry in the old customary ways. Some people *had* to ignore the Act since their religious beliefs prevented them from marrying according to Anglican rites. Others, especially Roman Catholics, simply did not see the necessity of a second legal ceremony. The net result was the same: such unions were no longer legally valid and those who entered into them ensured, whether knowingly or unknowingly, that their children would be bastards.

There were other rules governing the legality of marriages. Most of them were designed to prevent marriages between close blood relations such as siblings, aunt and nephew, uncle and niece. Marriages between first cousins were prohibited until the Reformation. The 'forbidden degrees' followed the rules laid down in *Leviticus*, 18, but they were also held to extend to the spiritual affinity (god-parents) and, on the principle that marriage united husband and wife as one person, to other non-blood relationships such as marriages between step-parent and step-child and marriages between a widow and her husband's brother or between a widower and his wife's sister. Before the Reformation it was possible to obtain a papal dispensation to waive the rules, but it was the right to issue such dispensations that was at the heart of the Reformation in England. Henry VIII had obtained just such a dispensation in order to marry Catherine of Aragon, who had previously been married to his deceased brother. When Henry wanted to challenge the legality of his marriage to Catherine, he alleged that the dispensation was invalid.

After the Reformation, church law in England continued to be distinct from common law but it was administered by courts that acknowledged the crown rather than the pope as head of the church and of the church court system. The 'forbidden degrees' were defined in the Book of Common Prayer. The principle that they extended to non-blood relationships also continued. Some people were married either in defiance or in ignorance of these rules, but such marriages were technically incestuous and therefore void – though whether, in practice, challenges were made remains unclear. In the nineteenth century there was a high-profile campaign to legalise marriage between a man and his deceased wife's sister, and this particular bar was abolished by act of Parliament in 1907 (although marriages between a husband and his *divorced* wife's sister remained invalid). Further statutory changes to the forbidden degrees were made in 1921 and 1931, and are now defined by the Marriage Act of 1949. However the most common reason for declaring a marriage to be void was the discovery that it was bigamous. Getting married was easy; getting divorced was almost impossible.

6. Divorce, separation, re-marriage and cohabitation

Until 1858, the options available to couples whose marriages broke down were limited. Separating couples could bring a matrimonial suit in the ecclesiastical courts. A successful suit had three possible outcomes:

*   The marriage could be annulled on the grounds that it was either void (illegal from the outset because it was bigamous, incestuous, or for lack of consent) or voidable (a marriage that was valid until challenged, for example where one or both of the parties was under the age of marriage).
*   The court could issue an order of jactitation: essentially a statement that no marriage had taken place.
*   The grant of a divorce from bed and board *(a mensa et a thoro)*.

A void marriage was one that had never – in law at least – existed. Although the parties may have believed themselves to be married, they were not and therefore retained the right to act as though they were single: someone whose marriage was void, for example, could not be convicted of bigamy. A voidable marriage was quite different: it remained legally valid until challenged (which might, in early times, have been after the deaths of the parties concerned). Until the fifteenth century, if the parents did not know of an impediment to their marriage, then their children would remain legitimate even if the marriage were annulled; thereafter until the law was changed in the twentieth century the children of any marriage that had been annulled were bastardised.

However decrees made by the church courts might not be accepted by the common law courts (especially if it could be proved that the decree had been obtained collusively). Elizabeth Chudleigh married Augustus Hervey secretly in 1744. Their relationship broke down in 1747 and in 1769 she obtained a decree of jactitation. The suit was almost certainly collusive since both she and Hervey were anxious to remarry. She married the Duke of Kingston and lived with him as his wife until his death in 1773. The validity of her second marriage was then called into doubt and, the decree of jactitation not withstanding, she was convicted of bigamy in 1776 after one of the most spectacular trials of the century (she was tried in the House of Lords).

The third option, a divorce from bed and board, did not affect the legitimacy of the children, but it did not amount to a divorce in the sense that we now understand it. During the sixteenth century, in the aftermath of the Reformation, the legal status of a church divorce was unclear. Some people believed that it permitted the parties to remarry, others that it was merely a way of formalizing a separation. A decision in the court of Star Chamber in 1602 clarified the position: a church divorce did not dissolve a marriage, it merely provided what we would now call a judicial separation. Perhaps as a result of this legacy of uncertainty, when Parliament acted to criminalise bigamy in 1603 (before that date it was merely an offence against church law) it specifically excluded remarriage after a church divorce.

The only legal way of dissolving a marriage in England and Wales was to obtain a divorce by private act of Parliament; the first such act was passed in 1670 and dissolved the marriage of Lord Roos [32]. Parliamentary divorce was not only expensive, it was also extremely difficult. In order to obtain one, a male petitioner had to establish his wife's adultery; a female had to establish not only that her husband was adulterous but that he had also committed some other marital crime. In practice, therefore, it was easier for a man to apply for a divorce than for a woman, and most successful petitioners were male.

By the end of the eighteenth century, Parliament generally required the divorce bill to be preceded by not one but by two legal actions. One of these was a suit known as 'criminal conversation' ('crim. con.' for short) in which the wronged husband sued his wife's lover for damages for their adultery [31]. The second was an action in the church courts for a divorce from bed and board. Some applications for a parliamentary divorce were collusive: that is, the wife had agreed to provide the appropriate evidence to enable her husband to win the actions in the lower courts and thus to obtain a

Then, in order to prove a particular Fact, called *Mary Parker*, who being sworn, acquainted the House, " That she knows Mr. *Williams* and his Wife; was their " Servant: That Mrs. *Lantware* hired her in *October* " 1773 : That she lived with them about Three Months : " That Mrs. *Williams* was always out, and brought " home Men in an Evening when her Master was in " Bed : That she came home dressed and painted often " at Three o'Clock in the Morning, and her Cloaths " always ruffled. When her Master came home he used " to ask for his Wife: That she told him she was with " her Mother: That Men came often to ask for Mrs. " *Williams*: That her Master knocked at the Door, and " a Man was sent into the Kitchen: That her Master " went out of Town in the Beginning of the Year " 1774, when One Man came and staid all Night, and " did so Two or Three different Times: That she was " sent by her Mistress for Beer, and when she returned, " observed a Man under the Bed, and another Time a " Man in the Dining Room: That she thought her " Mistress knocked, and upon her going up she found " a Man upon her Mistress upon the Floor: That she " believes her Master did not know of these goings on : " That when she went up into the Dining Room, be- " sides what she has already mentioned, her Mistress " was on the Carpet, her Cloaths up, and a Man upon " her: That her Mistress had her Cloaths on, but they " were up: She left the Door open, and about an Hour " after he went away: That Mr. *Williams* knew of this " Conduct of his Wife about *January*, when he used " to follow her to see where she went: That he went " out of Town, and left her, when she stripped the " House and went away: That she did not tell her " Master of what passed, as she did not like to make " Mischief: That she did not know the Man who lay " upon her Mistress: That one *Birch* came there, whom " her Mistress said, " she would go and live with ;" nor " did she know any other of the Men who frequented " her Mistress."

She was directed to withdraw.

Plate 1. Divorce by Act of Parliament, 1775. Thomas Williams began proceedings in the House of Lords to divorce his wife, Ann Lantware, in September 1775. As was usual in such cases, the evidence, graphically reported in the Lords' Journal *concentrates on the wife's alleged adultery. Source:* Lord's Journal, *September 1775*

parliamentary divorce. Others were bitterly contested. Costs naturally varied from case to case, but it is unlikely that they were ever less than several hundred pounds and they frequently ran into several thousands.

Not surprisingly those faced with the difficulty of obtaining a divorce at home sometimes tried to resolve the situation by obtaining one abroad. Divorce was available in every other protestant European country – including Scotland. Since Scottish *marriages* were recognised as legally binding by the English courts – even after Hardwicke's Marriage Act – it was only reasonable to suppose that Scottish *divorces* would also be recognised in England. Since the Scots courts were reluctant to allow themselves to be used to remedy defects in English law, the number of couples who were able to take advantage of their services was small. This was fortunate, because in 1811 the English judges ruled that the loophole did not exist when they sentenced William Lolly to transportation for bigamy, even though he had obtained a divorce in Scotland before his remarriage. It took extensive high-level negotiations before common sense prevailed and his sentence was commuted.

Another way of ending a marriage was provided by the folk custom of wife sale. The objective was to obtain public recognition of the dissolution of one relationship and the start of another. A wife sale consisted of a ritual handing over of legal and financial obligations from one husband to another in return for what was usually a token sum of money. They are frequently recorded as having taken place in the cattle market on market day, but sales by written contract are also known. Unlike Thomas Hardy's fictional account in the *Mayor of Casterbridge* (1886) they did not result from decisions made on the whim of the moment, nor were the wives sold to strangers; they simply publicised a pre-arranged agreement between the three parties: the husband, the wife and her lover. A variation on this theme of public repudiation of the marriage was for the couple to jump backwards over a broomstick in a symbolic reversal of the wedding rite. Neither custom had any legal validity so any children of subsequent relationships would be illegitimate [37].

The easiest, cheapest and most common way of ending a marriage was a separation. From the late seventeenth century onwards, some wealthier couples formalised their parting by means of a private deed of separation [31; 41]. In the absence of a parliamentary divorce there could be no legal remarriage, but that did not prevent bigamy or cohabitation. Where one or both partners were geographically mobile it would be difficult for anyone in the new community to know about marital status. This might mean either that it would be easy to marry bigamously (perhaps unknown even to the new partner) or that a couple could cohabit without anyone realising that they were not legally married. Until the late nineteenth century, criminal prosecutions were brought, organised and paid for by private individuals – usually the victim. If those most concerned with the situation were happy with it, or if only a small number of people knew the truth, then the chances of a prosecution were pretty small. Even if charges were brought, evidence of a separation of seven years and a genuine belief that one's partner was dead constituted a good defence.

Legislation to facilitate divorce in England came into effect in 1858 [32]. The legislation of 1858 also abolished criminal conversation as an action, substituting a new action for damages against the wife's 'seducer' and allowing the sum awarded to be divided between the wife, children and husband at the discretion of the judge [31]. By 1861 the number of divorces granted had risen from around about 4 a year to approximately 150. By 1914 over 800 people were getting divorced every year. The increase may seem to have been huge, but statistically it was tiny – divorce affected fewer than one in a thousand married couples. The grounds for divorce were still restricted, following the requirements that had already been established for a parliamentary divorce: adultery by the wife, or adultery by the husband coupled with another marital offence. Divorce was certainly cheaper after 1858 than before, but it was still outside the reach of most ordinary people. A few did save up for one, but most continued to separate and to form new partnerships by means of bigamous marriages or cohabitation just as before. From 1878 separations could be formalised by obtaining a separation and maintenance order from the local magistrates.

The debates over divorce – whether it did or did not encourage immorality and whether it should or should not be made more easily accessible – continued to be acrimonious, but they took place against a background of continuing changes in society and its attitudes to divorce and sexuality. The divorce rate rose rapidly during and immediately after the First World War, eventually stabilising at a level about four times higher than before the war. In part this was because the grounds for divorce were equalised in 1923, allowing wives greater access to divorce. In part it was because the introduction of legal aid had made divorce more accessible to the lower middle classes.

In 1937, the Divorce Reform Act (largely based on the recommendations of a Royal Commission of 1912) extended grounds for divorce to include desertion for three years, cruelty and habitual drunkenness. Within two years the number of divorces rose by nearly 175%. The outbreak of the Second World War sent them up still higher: there were just over 8,000 divorces in 1939; by 1947 there were about 60,000. The figures then began to stabilise but never returned to pre-war levels, largely because the legal aid reforms of 1948 effectively made divorce available to the poor for the first time. Over 90% of divorce applications were uncontested but there still remained a substantial number of marriages that could not be ended because of the refusal of one of the parties to proceed. In the late 1960s it was estimated that some 200,000 children had been born to couples unable to marry because of the restrictive nature of the divorce laws. The current 'no fault' divorce laws were introduced in 1971.

7. Sexual exploitation

So far we have considered procreation in terms of courtship and either marriage or stable cohabitation, but some of the children concerned were conceived outside such relationships. Sexual violence and exploitation were as much part of our ancestors' lives as of our own. Rape was a capital offence until the early nineteenth century, but it was difficult to secure a conviction since the legal definition of rape made it necessary to establish both penetration and emission within the victim's body. Male attitudes to female sexuality and chastity made it difficult for them to distinguish between seduction and rape, and since all jurors were male and those men who went to trial almost inevitably defended themselves on grounds of consent, the acquittal rate was high. George Carter, tried at the Old Bailey in 1772 for rape, was one of those who were acquitted. His sixteen-year-old maid testified that he raped her on the first night that she spent in his house and that his wife subsequently told her that he served all his maidservants so. Sadly it is not a particularly unusual story. Contemporary testimony, often gathered in the course of an enquiry into some completely unrelated event, does make it clear that for some women – particularly lower-class ones – rape was a common hazard of life.

Sometimes one suspects that a particular union may have been consensual but nevertheless part of a very uneven power relationship, in which sex was traded for other advantages. Perhaps the most extreme example of this occurred in the household of Lord Mansfield, the famous judge. Mansfield's nephew, Sir John Lindsay, was a naval officer who had an affair with a slave girl whom he found on board a captured ship. It is hard to believe that this affair could have been anything other than exploitative, since the slave girl was not in a position to reject his advances, and granting sexual favours probably bought her a far more comfortable life. Yet for all this, Lindsay seems to have been genuinely smitten. When she became pregnant, he could have abandoned her, but he did not. When she died, he could have abandoned the baby, but he did not. The infant Dido Elizabeth Belle was raised and educated in Lord Mansfield's household. Despite her unique combination of disadvantages (being female, black, illegitimate and a slave), she grew up to be a forceful young lady and at Mansfield's death received her freedom and a substantial legacy. Her mother's fate, however, is mirrored in the experiences of many others who became the mistresses of their employers or of their employers' sons, brothers, nephews and friends. For hundreds, perhaps thousands, of servant girls, sexual exploitation came as part of the job description, though we should not forget that it was not uncommon for a man to pay lip service to convention by passing off his mistress as his housekeeper, just as some women passed their lovers off as lodgers.

The range of sexual behaviours exhibited in the past is likely to have been very similar to our own day. Then, as now, there were incidents in which females were violently raped by strangers. Then, as now, some females were sexually abused by male relatives or by men with whom they had a quasi-incestuous relationship: stepfathers, stepbrothers, and lodgers. Then, as now, some children were conceived as a result of sexual services bought with goods or hard cash. Then, as now, some men took advantage of girls who were vulnerable by reason of emotional stress or mental illness, or whose mental development was too retarded for them to have any real appreciation of the consequences of their actions. Then, as now, some girls entered into sexual relationships with the deliberate intention of enticing their partners into a deeper and longer-term commitment than originally envisaged.

8. Becoming an unmarried mother

For an upper-class unmarried girl to become pregnant was always a matter for deep shame, and this attitude was increasingly transmitted down through the social classes. In the mid eighteenth century, Sussex shopkeeper Thomas Turner was deeply shocked to discover that his neighbour had become a father after only six months of marriage. A century later similar attitudes were becoming characteristic of working-class men too, with distressing consequences for daughters who threatened to disgrace the family. In London in 1875, fourteen-year-old Rose Carey was disowned by her father and quite literally turned out of the house when he discovered her pregnancy. There must have been many like her, but we know about Rose Carey in more detail because she subsequently fought and won a child custody case which established new rights for single mothers.

Of course, there were parents who were prepared to offer tangible support, occasionally causing considerable affront to supercilious social investigators in the process by describing their unmarried pregnant daughters as merely 'misfortunate'. Some were prepared to brazen things out. Others tried to conceal the truth. This might involve sending the pregnant girl on an extended 'holiday' to conceal both the expanding waistline and the birth, then either arranging for the child to be cared for by someone else or deciding that the girl's mother should pass off the new baby as her own rather than her daughter's. The author Catherine Cookson was not the only child to discover that her older sister was actually her mother. Where sources (like the census) permit it, always look carefully at the family relationships given.

The first institution created specifically for unmarried mothers appears to have been the Dalston Refuge which was opened in London in 1805. Others soon followed. Admission to such homes was sometimes voluntary, sometimes not. The homes existed to reform the 'fallen' mothers and to return them to society as useful, moral citizens, rather than to provide support for them and their children. It was taken for granted that the mothers would be permanently separated from their babies. Although we may now find it very difficult to understand why this was thought to be desirable, it is important to realise that it was done with the best of intentions. It was thought to be in the mother's interests (as well as that of society) that she be deterred from re-offending. It was also in the child's best interests that it be removed from moral contamination and brought up in a disciplined institutional environment; single mothers were by definition immoral ones and their children were better off without them. The first mother and baby home that actually permitted and encouraged mothers to keep and care for their babies was not created until 1871, and even then its name, the Female Mission to the Fallen, provides a powerful reminder of the social opprobrium attached to single mothers.

Children are expensive. They require food and clothing. They also require care and attention of a kind that limits the mother's earning capacity. Much depended on the economic structure and prosperity of the neighbourhood, and it is entirely possible that in prosperous times in areas where outwork was still the industrial norm or where there were other opportunities for regular homeworking, single (and married) mothers may well have been able to combine work and motherhood in ways that we can no longer envisage. Mother and baby homes of the kind described above provided temporary accommodation only. It was not until the twentieth century (starting with the foundation of the London Day Servants Hostel in 1912) that any attempt was made to provide unmarried mothers with permanent accommodation that would allow them to keep their children and ease themselves back into the employment market. For the most part therefore, single mothers who were going to keep their babies needed some form of child maintenance agreement. Your chances of tracing some information about one will depend on the date of the birth and the laws governing maintenance orders (also known as bastardy or affiliation orders) at that time [24]. But remember that if the father was willing to meet his obligations then a private agreement might suffice, and that such agreements rarely survive.

9. Avoiding the problem: abortion and infanticide

Some unmarried girls were so fearful that they disguised their condition and attempted to deliver their babies unaided and in secret. Many found, perhaps to their relief, that their experience of single parenthood was brief, because their babies did not survive.

All the information we have indicates that in all periods, illegitimate children have been more likely to have poorer parents, to be underweight and to have more health problems and a higher infant mortality rate than legitimate ones. Illegitimate babies also ran a greater risk of arriving in this world significantly damaged by a failed abortion. Although abortion was illegal, herbal abortifacients were certainly available and, for those knowledgeable enough and brave enough to seek one out, there were a number of back-street abortionists. The abortionists themselves rarely appear in the records, unless they managed to kill the mother too, in which case there might be a prosecution for murder.

Discovering the body of a newborn was not particularly unusual. Many had clearly been killed to protect their mothers from shame: surviving assize records suggest that infanticide was the largest single category of murder and that illegitimate children were at greater risk of this than legitimate ones [30]. Most killings were attributable to the mother, but occasionally one discovers that other relatives were responsible. Attitudes to infanticide have changed significantly over time. In the late seventeenth century, society's horror at 'murdering mothers' led to tougher legislation and an increase in the number who were hanged, but the shock caused by the sight of a woman on the gallows meant that the courts soon became more lenient. Infant mortality was very high anyway, so unless the cause of death was obvious it was difficult to tell whether it was murder or not; sometimes it was impossible to be sure whether the baby had ever lived at all.

By the eighteenth century some doctors were willing to give scientific testimony about this. If the baby's lungs floated in water then the child had been born alive. If they did not, then it had been stillborn. Jurors tended to be sceptical about this test, and were therefore left heavily dependent on interpreting circumstantial evidence. Concealment of birth became a serious offence in its own right, since it suggested an intent to dispose of the child. Conversely, a mother who had prepared for the birth, however secretly, by collecting together a set of baby clothes, was likely to gain the benefit of the doubt. By the twentieth century, the condition that we now call post-natal depression had been recognised and in 1922 infanticide was created as a crime in its own right. It is defined as the killing of a child under the age of 12 months by its own mother whilst the balance of her mind is disturbed by failure to recover fully from childbirth or from the effects of lactation. It is no longer categorised as murder but as a form of manslaughter.

Continuing anxiety about the fate of illegitimate babies, and suspicions that unscrupulous midwives and maternity home proprietors colluded in disposing of live babies after declaring them to be stillborn, led in 1926 to the requirement that stillbirths be registered.

10. Child maintenance: the role of the medieval church courts

It was once thought that there were no clear rules about who should maintain an illegitimate child before the sixteenth century: that child support was a matter for the immediate family and for charity. However, recent research, especially by Helmholz [16] has shown that although the common law did not provide any mechanism by which a father could be made to support his bastard child, church law did recognise the obligation of parents to support all their children, whether legitimate or illegitimate, and that this obligation was enforced by the church courts. The duty was a reciprocal one: all children, whether legitimate or illegitimate, also had a duty to support their parents.

The church courts could take cognisance of a bastardy case in one of two ways: by petition of the mother on behalf of her child or by an *ex officio* prosecution for fornication or adultery that had resulted in the birth of a bastard child. An *ex officio* prosecution was one brought by some ecclesiastical officer, often a churchwarden. Documentation arising out of cases in which alleged ('putative') fathers were ordered to support their bastard children survives in nearly every ecclesiastical jurisdiction. In cases where the man denied paternity then the court would make an interim order pending some further investigation. The procedures adopted reflected a clear and deliberate intention to ensure that the child received immediate support even at the risk of being unfair to the man alleged to be the father. If at the preliminary hearing the mother could make a presumptive case against the putative father then he would be ordered to support the child until a full hearing could be held. At the full hearing, the court would rely on circumstantial evidence such as an admission of sexual relations and 'common fame' in the community, and would make a decision in accordance with the balance of probabilities. Sometimes the courts used a process called *compurgation*: that is they required the mother not only to testify on oath but to find oath helpers prepared to swear that they believed her testimony to be true and unperjured. In practice many cases (known in the church courts as causes) never went as far as a second hearing, probably because the judges encouraged litigants to come to a settlement. Where the father was too poor to take on the burden of support, other relatives might be ordered to do so. In theory, there was no upper limit on the amount that the father could be ordered to pay, since it was thought to be appropriate that the child support payments should reflect the father's means, but in practice it was usually put at one shilling [5p] a week.

The church courts also had procedures to deal with those who fell behind with their payments. Since supporting one's child was a moral duty, the courts were anxious to ensure that putative fathers not only undertook but willingly acknowledged their obligations. Accordingly, they were anxious to encourage arbitration and agreement. If this failed then they could impose their ultimate sanction: excommunication. In the worst cases excommunication could be 'signified' to Chancery which would result in the imprisonment of the defaulter by the sheriff, but the emphasis on voluntary agreement meant that this process was rarely invoked.

In 1576 [11] the justices of the peace (who acted under common law) were also empowered to investigate bastardy and issue maintenance orders. This did not signal the end of church court jurisdiction but simply provided an alternative (probably more accessible) venue for such actions.

11. Child maintenance: the poor law before 1834

After the dissolution of the monasteries (1536-40), responsibility for maintaining the poor, including destitute children, was increasingly concentrated in the parish. This close association of poor relief with the parish, meant that it was essential that both individuals and the parochial authorities should know to which parish they belonged, or in the language of the time, the parish in which they were settled. Rights of settlement could be acquired in a number of ways, including birth, apprenticeship, payment of poor rates and renting property over £10. Women acquired their husband's settlement on marriage.

People who moved from one parish to another were often asked to provide evidence of their parish of settlement which was done by means of interviews that were recorded in writing (known as examinations) and sometimes they were asked to obtain a 'certificate' from their parish of settlement. The certificate amounted to a legally binding agreement between the parish of settlement and the parish of residence that the parish of settlement would pay up if and when this person ever needed poor relief (known as becoming 'chargeable'). It covered not only the individual but also his family, including children as yet unborn. Such certificates facilitated migration and were highly prized. Although they were often handed over to the authorities in the new parish, some people preferred to keep them, and may still survive in the possession of their descendants. Some parishes assumed that a certificate also covered unborn illegitimate children, but in 1742 the courts decided that the principle of 'no one's child' put bastards outside the system: just as an illegitimate child had no right to inherit its parents' goods, so it had no right to inherit a settlement. Illegitimate children were settled where they were born.

The parochial authorities identified bastardy as a serious problem. This was more a matter of pragmatism than morality. Illegitimate children were more likely to end up destitute than legitimate ones. Once again the principle of 'no one's child' created complications, since it meant that under common law neither parent actually had a legal obligation to maintain the child (nor for that matter did they have a legal right to custody of the child). Furthermore the common law courts had no legal mechanism to ensure that pregnant single girls identified the father or to force him to make maintenance payments until this was specifically authorised by statute in 1576. Such orders could not be enforced against men in the armed services.

From 1610 'lewd' women unable to maintain an illegitimate child could be imprisoned for up to a year. A repeat offence could lead to indefinite imprisonment (though it is not known ever to have done so). Either (or both) parents might be sentenced to a whipping at courts of quarter sessions. From 1662, the parish was able to confiscate the parents' goods if they absconded leaving the child chargeable, and parochial powers were further strengthened by an act of 1732 which required pregnant single girls to identify the father under oath. Failure to do so was punishable by imprisonment. If no identification was forthcoming, it was the duty of the village midwife to put pressure on unmarried girls during the birth to secure one. Following the established procedures of the church courts [10], very little corroborative evidence was required, and the onus was on the accused man to prove his innocence. The potential for abuse was obvious. It was alleged that unscrupulous women used their pregnancies to blackmail innocent men or that they simply named the man who seemed most likely to be able to afford the maintenance payments. Occasionally such allegations were substantiated, but since disputed orders could be appealed to quarter sessions, and since justices were not quite as gullible as we would sometimes like to think, it is on the whole unlikely that this was common practice.

It was in the ratepayers' interests to make sure that as few bastards as possible were born in their parish and that there were sound child maintenance arrangements in place to provide for those who were born there. To this end, parochial officers adopted two basic strategies. The first was to encourage, forcibly or otherwise, non-resident pregnant single women to give birth elsewhere. Hence the ubiquity of entries in churchwardens' accounts recording payments to get 'big-bellied' women across the border into another parish, although from 1732 it became illegal for women to be subjected to compulsory removal during pregnancy and for a month after the birth.

The second strategy was to ensure that the father acknowledged his responsibilities. There were several possible objectives. One was to persuade the couple to marry. This not only ensured the child's legitimacy, it could also provide an insurance against future problems. Once married, a woman changed her settlement to that of her husband – so there was a possibility that responsibility for any future welfare payments could be off-loaded to another parish. Some marriages were encouraged with threats, others with offers to cover the cost of the ceremony and additional cash incentives. If marriage was not a realistic or useful solution to the problem, the parish might seek a legal order to force the father to make regular maintenance payments (usually a shilling [5p] a week), or a one-off capital payment to the parish or a legally binding agreement (bond) to indemnify the parish against future expense.

All this meant that the parish needed to identify and record the fathers of illegitimate children and/or to punish those parents who were unable or unwilling to support their illegitimate offspring. This involved a certain amount of surveillance of pregnant women and the production of extensive (and informative) documentation for those known or suspected to be single [**39**].

12. Child maintenance: the poor law after 1834

The Poor Law Amendment Act of 1834 (often know as the 'New' Poor Law) was introduced at a time of economic depression and high unemployment by legislators who were extremely worried about what we now call 'welfare dependency'. It was intended to encourage the able-bodied poor to seek work rather than welfare, by forcing those who did ask for help into workhouses, where the conditions were made deliberately harsh and families were separated from one another. The objective was to abolish 'out-relief' (payments of money that enabled the poor to remain in the community) in favour of 'in-relief' (admission to the workhouse). The Act also created a new local government unit to help administer the poor law by grouping parishes into units large enough to make the building of a workhouse viable. These new Poor Law Unions were run by elected authorities called Boards of Guardians. You can get an excellent idea of just how daunting these places were from the workhouse website [**46**]. In practice the giving of out-relief continued in a number of areas for decades, but it is difficult to generalise and by the later nineteenth century, there were certainly a number of Unions where out-relief had virtually ceased.

The legislators were not just concerned about unemployment, they believed that the existing poor law system encouraged bastardy. They regarded the payment of child maintenance directly to the mother as a form of income, and were concerned that there was no way of ensuring that payments made for the support of the child were actually used for that purpose. They also argued that it was wrong that a poor unmarried mother should be financially more independent than a respectable widow: to quote the report of the poor law commissioners (1834), 'A base-born child should be a burden to its mother, as Providence evidently intended'. Traditionally, pregnant single girls had been encouraged to marry the putative father, but this too was now seen as a grievous error, one that led to early, improvident marriages and an increase in the number of pauper children (albeit legitimate ones). Bastardy, in their eyes, was not simply a problem for individuals and their families, but was a threat to society as a whole.

The 1834 Act repealed the existing provisions for bastardy and transferred all liability for the maintenance of illegitimate children to the mother. The payment of out-relief to unmarried mothers was prohibited. The mother had no legal redress against a father who refused to make maintenance payments, but if as a result of this the child became chargeable, the poor law authorities were able to sue him at quarter sessions. The mother's testimony was crucial to obtaining the order, but it now required corroboration. The sum to be paid by the father could not exceed the actual cost of the maintaining the child and no money recovered from the father could be paid to the mother or spent on her. The reasoning was clear: only by refusing to pay for the confinement of single mothers or for the maintenance of their children could society punish them sufficiently to deter others from illicit sex and pregnancy. If the ratepayers were going to have to support illegitimate children through childhood, then they had a right to remove them from their morally defective mothers, and thereby to give them a better chance to grow up into respectable, responsible citizens. It follows that for this period the records of the poor law authorities should always be one of the first ports of call [40].

13. Child maintenance: affiliation orders after 1844

By abolishing the mother's right to child maintenance, the terms of the 1834 Act probably removed a great deal of her bargaining power. Before 1834, mothers had nothing to lose by seeking poor relief and threatening to do so gave them an additional negotiating tool to use against fathers who were reluctant to pay maintenance. After 1834 this was no longer so. Not surprisingly, the system was soon abolished. In 1844 a new system of affiliation proceedings was introduced. Control was returned to the mother (or other person having custody) who could apply for a maintenance order either before the birth of her child or up to a year after its birth [24]. Any application made later than that would fail without proof that the father had contributed towards the child's maintenance during the first year of its life.

The mother could also apply for costs. In the mid to late nineteenth century, these might range from a few shillings, if professional legal advice was not required, to a guinea (21 shillings in old money or £1.05 in decimal coinage) for a solicitor and perhaps two further guineas for a barrister. Payments could be up to five shillings (25p) a week for the first six weeks and two shillings and sixpence (12.5p) thereafter plus up to ten shillings (50p) for the midwife's costs and a similar amount for the cost of a burial if necessary. Certain features of the pre-1834 system remained in place. Although the 1844 Act and subsequent legislation specifically referred to a 'single woman', the judges continued to hold (as they had done since the early eighteenth century) that married mothers of illegitimate children were single for the purposes of the Act. Liability to pay maintenance ceased on the death of the father, and because of the *filius nullius* rule could not be enforced against his estate.

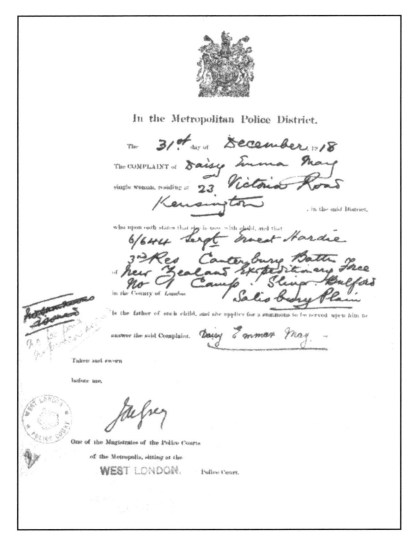

In the Metropolitan Police District.

The 31st day of December, 19 18

The COMPLAINT of Daisy Emma May

single woman, residing at 23 Victoria Road
Kensington , in the said District,

who upon oath states that she is now with child, and that
6/6444 Sergt Ernest Hardie
3rd Res Canterbury Battn of
New Zealand Expeditionary Force
No 9 Camp Sling Bulford
in the County of London Salisbury Plain

is the father of such child, and she applies for a summons to be served upon him to
answer the said Complaint. Daisy Emma May

Taken and sworn

before me,

One of the Magistrates of the Police Courts
of the Metropolis, sitting at the
WEST LONDON. Police Court.

Plate 2. Application for an affiliation order, 1918. The annotation indicates
that no summons was actually issued in this case, so perhaps there was a
happy ending. The applicant's signature, like so many others in this wartime
volume, suggests that she may have been very young.
Source: LMA, PS.WLN/B3/1 Crown Copyright

28

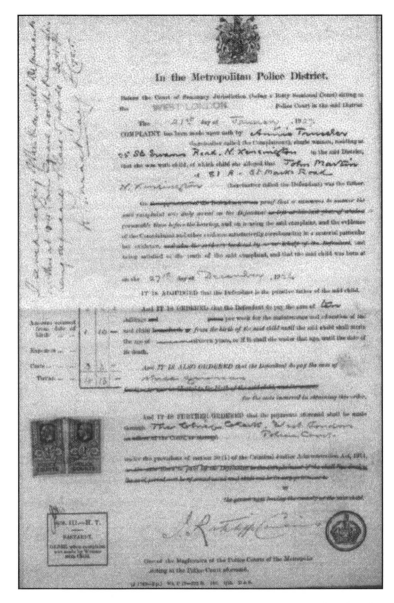

Plate 3. Affiliation order, 1926. Note the wealth of information this form provides: the full names and addresses of both parents, details of costs, and some valuable extras - the annotation at the top left hand corner not only gives us the address of the paternal grandmother, it even gives the name and warrant number of the policeman who served the order. Source: LMA, PS.WLN/B3/1 Crown Copyright

An application for a maintenance order had to be made to the petty sessional division or other jurisdiction local to the mother's residence. At the hearing the mother's evidence had to be corroborated to the satisfaction of the justices – a somewhat elastic requirement falling far short of satisfaction beyond all reasonable doubt. Circumstantial evidence showing 'that the defendant has been seen with the woman under very suspicious circumstances, indicating close and indecent intimacy between them' or that the man had been treated as the father amounted to sound corroboration. So did any admission by the putative father that he had had sex with the mother.

The defences available to the alleged father were limited. No order could be granted if the birth had taken place abroad or if the alleged father was under 14, since the law presumed him to be incapable of intercourse, even if proof to the contrary could be provided. Arguing that the mother was unchaste was irrelevant, since that was already proven by her condition. In order to rebut the charge, the putative father needed to be able to show that there were other candidates for fatherhood, or that the mother was too unreliable to be believed. Even if he won, the mother could still bring another action. If he lost then he had a mere 24 hours in which to lodge notice of appeal. If he defaulted on his payments for a month his goods could be confiscated and sold, or (if he had no goods) he could be imprisoned.

In what was probably a reaction against the draconian legislation of 1834, the 1844 Act required that maintenance payments be made directly to the mother or to whomever had custody of the child, as long as the child was not actually chargeable. Mindful of the ever-present link between poverty and illegitimacy, the Act also required the justices to send a copy of the order to the clerk of the guardians of the poor for the area in which mother was resident at the time of the order was made [40].

Further clauses of the Act probably reflect the need to provide reassurance to those who feared any system of child maintenance payments would simply encourage higher levels of illegitimacy. It is perhaps understandable that the misuse of child support payments should be made into an offence (carrying a fine of up to £10). More intriguing is the requirement that each petty session should make an annual return of bastardy cases to the local clerk of the peace. These returns were to include full details of each case. Clerks of the peace were instructed to preserve such lists and transmit a certified copy to the Home Office together with a list of all cases appealed to quarter sessions, and the result of the appeal. Presumably this was to enable the Home Office to discover the existence of serial offenders – feckless individuals littering the country with illegitimate offspring – but without a computer it must have been extremely difficult to collate such a wealth of information and one finds it difficult to believe that Home Office officials even bothered to read them [26].

The broad framework introduced by the 1844 Act remained fundamentally unchanged until the creation of the Child Support Agency in the 1990s. Much of the detail, however, changed substantially over the years. The requirement for annual bastardy returns was dropped in 1858. From 1877 affiliation orders could be enforced against members of the armed forces. The weekly sum available was increased in 1866, again in 1919 and again in 1923 (when it reached £1 a week). Other changes made it easier to pursue defaulting fathers for arrears. The appeal mechanism was also altered – essentially returning to the pre-1834 situation in that appeals on the facts were heard by quarter sessions but appeals on points of law were determined by the judges of the superior courts. From 1866, the poor law authorities were once again allowed to apply for maintenance orders against putative fathers – but only if the child was actually chargeable. In the economic depression that characterised much of the later nineteenth century, arguments about welfare dependency resurfaced, resulting in another drive to eliminate the payment of out-relief. In areas where this policy was rigorously enforced, single women were once again forced into workhouses for their confinements, and those unable either to secure or to enforce maintenance payments from the father were likely to have their children removed [40].

By the early twentieth century, the intersection of moral outrage and of theories of eugenics meant that the problem of destitute unmarried mothers became identified as a mental health issue. Those who were certified as 'moral imbeciles' or 'moral defectives' were liable to be detained under the Mental Deficiency Act 1913.

Although the process of obtaining an order might seem reasonably straight forward to the layman, it provided considerable scope for legal argument and soon developed its own case law. Between the legislators and their propensity for piecemeal change and the lawyers with their propensity for discovering legal technicalities, it is not surprising that in 1936 the editor of the standard textbook, *Lushington's Law of Affiliation and Bastardy* was driven to comment that 'The bastardy law is a disgusting patchwork as it stands. I have done my best to make it intelligible'. If the precise details about who was entitled to apply for an order, and what their entitlement was, are important to you, then use the edition of Saunders or Lushington [45] that is as contemporaneous to your case as possible.

14. The unwanted child: (1) foundlings, baby farming and adoption

As indicated above, schemes to help single mothers keep their children were rare. What then of the mother who wished to work, but who lacked a supportive family/ community network, who was either unable to get a maintenance agreement or to get it enforced, or who wanted to wipe the slate clean and form a new relationship unencumbered by a child? As we have seen, for some mothers the solution was extreme: respectability could be redeemed by sacrificing the life of the baby or by pretending that it was a sibling. For others it became a question of finding someone else to take on the burden of childcare. In the provinces foundlings were relatively uncommon, but in London it was not unusual for babies or very young children to be found abandoned. Although many of them must have been illegitimate, others (perhaps especially those abandoned as toddlers) may have been abandoned because of poverty or widowhood. Unlike Henry Fielding's fictional *Tom Jones* (1749) who was brought up in the squire's house, such children were likely to be taken into parish care, where they would remain unless parentage could be established. Their names often reflect their foundling origins: many acquired the surname Temple, because they were found at the doors of London's Temple church; foundlings further to the west of London in St Clement Dane's often became Clement whilst those in St Dionis Backchurch became Dennis; in 1731, a baby found in the parish of Allhallows, Bread Street became Rachel Allhallows.

Although there were many orphanages in existence, their primary purpose was to care for the legitimate children of particular occupational or social groups. Thomas Coram's Foundling Hospital, established in 1741, was probably the first to admit the illegitimate. For a brief period between 1756 and 1760, encouraged by a government grant, it admitted all applicants but the mortality rate rose to such heights that the policy had to be abandoned. During the later nineteenth century there was ample scope for new charities, such as that founded by Dr Thomas Barnardo, to pitch in and rescue destitute and abandoned children.

Institutional carers such as poor law authorities and the Foundling Hospital coped with so many babies and children by putting them out to nurse. Some mothers made similar arrangements on a private basis. Foster parents expected to be paid either a weekly fee or a lump sum if they were expected to take a child permanently. In cold cash terms it can scarcely have been a particularly profitable transaction. If foster parents really did want to make a business of it, then clearly their profits would be higher if large numbers of children could be fostered with minimum expenditure on food, heating and clothing, or if they were able to collect a lump sum for a child who failed to survive. Women who agreed to foster children became objects of deep suspicion in almost every century: Thomas Coram and Jonas Hanway were following a familiar line when they attributed high infant mortality rates amongst nurse children to deliberate negligence and accused parish officers of conniving at the deaths to protect their ratepayers. Single mothers who used foster parents, or baby farmers as they were often known, were accused of conniving at the death of their children.

Baby farmers have a bad name. Some of them undoubtedly deserved it, being both callous and financially grasping; others were mentally disturbed and chose to foster children as a way of securing a supply of victims for sadistic and perverted purposes; some were simply incompetent. There was certainly a trickle of scandals that confirmed people's worst suspicions about them. Perhaps the most infamous was that of Amelia Dyer whose activities were revealed when a bargeman fished a child's corpse from the Thames in the spring of 1896. The child had been strangled with tape and thrown into the river bundled in used wrapping paper. The wrapping paper still bore Mrs Dyer's address and, although she had moved, she was soon traced. By the time of her trial, seven other bodies had been found, all strangled with tape and wrapped in parcels: 'You'll know all mine' she is supposed to have said, 'by the tape around their necks'. At the time of her arrest and trial she had been baby farming for some 15 years, and scores of children must have passed through her hands. Whether she had been systematically killing them for the whole of that period or whether the murders were committed during a shorter period of stress/insanity are questions that have never been answered.

Amelia Dyer was hanged. So too, in 1870, was Margaret Walters, convicted of killing 16 babies left in her care. Other lesser scandals emerged from time to time. It is undeniable that many foster children lived in squalor and were under-nourished and under-stimulated. But in an age when malnutrition was rife, when most people lived in conditions we would now consider to be overcrowded and squalid, and when the use of laudanum and other drugs to keep babies quiet was commonplace, one can scarcely expect anything very different. Baby farmers were not all bad: they were impelled by a variety of motives, and enrichment was not necessarily the most important of them. Then as now a substantial minority of couples living in stable monogamous unions were struggling to reconcile their longing for a child with the realisation that they were infertile. Baby farming offered them a chance to adopt. Since in those days there were more unwanted babies than couples to take them, it was taken for granted that a 'premium' would be paid to the adoptive parents.

Amelia Dyer and Margaret Walters show us one side of the baby farming story. An otherwise obscure couple called Mr and Mrs Nash show us another. They were baby farmers who, in 1876, agreed to care for the baby daughter of a young single mother in return for regular weekly payments. We have already met the mother, Rose Carey, who was thrown out of the family home at the age of 14 when her pregnancy was discovered [8]. Rose Carey made some payments to the Nashes, but defaulted during a period of illness. She later became (in the words of her contemporaries) 'the kept mistress of a gentleman' and with her finances now established on a more secure basis, attempted to regain custody of her daughter. Mr and Mrs Nash refused to part with her. In 1880 Rose Carey began legal proceedings against them for detaining her child illegally. Her case was thrown out: the child was *filius nullius* so she had no rights. In 1882 she tried and failed again. She appealed to the divisional court and won her case, partly because she made it clear that she did not want custody for herself, but wanted the child to live with her (respectable) married sister. The Nashes then fought (and lost) the case in the Court of Appeal.

The problem faced by the Nashes – and many others – was that until 1927 there was no legal mechanism by which the birth mother could transfer full parental rights to adoptive parents. Most adopted or baby farmed children were illegitimate so adoptive parents could gain some protection from the *filius nullius* rule, since that meant the birth mother had no rights either. However, Rose Carey's case, decided in 1883, began to chip away at this. The rights of single mothers were further strengthened in 1891, when the House of Lords delivered its verdict in *Barnardo v McHugh*. Margaret McHugh's illegitimate son was found, apparently in a condition of destitution, and taken to one of Dr Barnardo's homes. Margaret McHugh subsequently signed an agreement to leave him in Barnardo's care until he was 21 years old. When she was prevented from visiting, she changed her mind and asked for his return. Barnardo refused, probably because of religious hostility (he was a committed protestant and Margaret McHugh was a Roman Catholic). The House of Lords declared that the agreement with Barnardo was invalid and the child was returned to his mother.

The *McHugh* decision confirmed that no contract or agreement transferring custody or parental rights from the birth mother to adoptive parents or other carers could be enforced at law. The result was that neither the birth mother nor the adoptive parents could ever be sure that the other party would keep the bargain. Nor could the child gain any rights: if the adoptive parents died intestate, the child would not be entitled to any inheritance from them or to be maintained out of their estate. This did not change until 1 January 1927 when the Adoption Act came into force. It is a measure of the unhappiness and uncertainty that surrounded adoptions before that date that the courts were immediately overwhelmed with applications for orders under the new Act.

The Adoption Act created, for the first time, a legally enforceable mechanism for the transfer of parental rights. Certificates of adoption were issued which replaced the original birth record. Although the act ensured that an adoption record could be linked to the birth record, it was thought to be best for all concerned that the break with the birth family be total, so this information was kept secret. More recently, it has been recognised that adopted children may wish to know about their origins, and since 1975 it has become possible for adopted children to have access to their birth records. All those adopted before 12 November 1975 must go through a process of counselling. Arrangements exist to provide counselling abroad for adopted persons who no longer live in the UK. The adopted person will also be supplied with sufficient information to trace the records of the court that made the adoption order and of the children's society or local authority (if any) that arranged the adoption [23]. The Registrar General also maintains an Adoption Contact Register in which birth parents, adoptees and other close relatives may (for a fee) enter their details (or those of an agreed intermediary). The support group NORCAP (National Organisation for Counselling Adoptees and their Parents) also maintains a contact register.

The legislation regarding access to birth records applies only to adoptees, but other relatives and descendants may apply under the terms of the 1958 Adoption Act to the court named on the copy of the entry in the Adopted Children Register. The application should be made in writing to the Chief Clerk of the court concerned.

Both before and after 1927, there were a variety of ways of making contact with potential foster or adoptive parents: personal knowledge and recommendation; the intervention of a sympathetic intermediary such as a priest, doctor, solicitor or midwife; newspaper adverts. Some adoption/fostering arrangements were set up by children's charities or by the poor law authorities. Where records survive they may well be extremely informative – containing much information about social background, including the name of the alleged father [42]. Records created and held by institutions (especially those that existed over a long period of time) obviously survive better than those that relate to purely private transactions, but be prepared for the possibility that no records may survive at all. If you are attempting to trace natural parents who lived in the twentieth century, or who may still be alive, you may find it useful to read a book on tracing missing persons, such as that by Rogers [45].

15. The unwanted child: (2) parochial apprenticeships and child emigration schemes

The scale of the problem of unwanted and destitute children worsened in the nineteenth century, not just because single mothers were increasingly discouraged from keeping their children but also for the very simple reason that improvements in hygiene and sanitation reduced the child mortality rate. The question of how best to care for those children who were not adopted and to ensure that the cycle of immorality was broken so that they became responsible adults and useful citizens was thus a major preoccupation of philanthropists and the poor law authorities.

Plate 4. Workhouse children in London, 1905. The photograph was taken as part of an attempt to publicise Ellinor Close's scheme to send groups of children to grow up on farms in suitable colonies. These children are probably all of a similar age, between 10 and 12 years old. Ellinor Close wanted to transfer much younger children (between 3 and 9 years of age) to 'small farms belonging to England, managed by English ladies, maintained by English money.' Since the children were free to return to England at the age of 14 or 16, this did not count as a fully fledged emigration scheme. The children (from left to right) are: unknown, James Davis, Sophy Green, Percy Murray, William Macastrine, George Murray, Amy White, Harry Macastrine, Arthur Osborne, P Rudman. Source: LMA, 20.61 A-DUR

Under the old poor law, the authorities were always keen to ensure that destitute children in their care were apprenticed. This was partly because apprenticeship was a recognised means of obtaining what we would now call a technical education. In practice, of course, the poor law authorities were rarely able or willing to pay the sort of fee (usually known as a 'premium') that was necessary to apprentice children to top rate tradesmen and many parochial apprenticeships were for relatively unskilled occupations. The other reason was that apprenticeship was one of the ways of changing an individual's settlement. By apprenticing children to masters in other areas, the authorities ensured that they had also off-loaded any future liability for poor relief [**25**].

By the late eighteenth century, the rise of the cotton industry in the North led to increasing labour shortages there. The recruitment of pauper apprentices provided an obvious solution, and before long children were being brought to the cotton mills from distant towns and cities, including London. It was a solution that seemed to have clear benefits for all: the employers obtained workers; the children obtained employment, a new parish of settlement and the chance of a better life away from the corrupting influences of their families; the parish of origin was freed of all obligations. The reality was rather different. Many of the children found themselves living and working under conditions of virtual slavery and were treated with considerable cruelty; even those who were treated kindly must have suffered from being removed at a very young age from all that was familiar to them. In 1816 Parliament acted to protect them, and, except in exceptional circumstances, apprenticing children against their own wishes or against the wishes of their parents or more than 40 miles from their home parish was forbidden.

The opportunities available to those caring for unwanted children expanded along with the Empire. Just like those long distance parish apprenticeships, shipping young people off to places like Australia, New Zealand, Canada and South Africa seemed to be one of those solutions that genuinely benefited everyone. The mother country was rid of a financial burden, but her children were being sent to strengthen the Empire and provide it with much needed (white) workers. The children were to benefit by being removed from English cities where their moral and physical health was under constant threat and being offered instead the opportunity to build a new life in a new society. As with the long distance apprenticeships, there was little or no appreciation of the psychological damage that might be inflicted on children forced to emigrate in this way, nor of the possibilities for physical and/or mental abuse in places sheltered from scrutiny. Emigration schemes, already permitted under the terms of the existing poor law, were extended in 1850 to children with no known parents or parish of settlement. Child emigration schemes were operated by almost all rescue charities and continued well into the middle of the twentieth century [40, 42].

You have only to look at the 'before and after' pictures reproduced here to appreciate how effective the propaganda could be. With hindsight we might wonder about the regimentation of the pose and the sheer lack of smiles, but what is known about the fate of two of the children in these photographs demonstrates just how difficult it is to make simplistic judgements about such complex issues. The children in the photographs were chosen because they all had health problems associated with poverty and malnutrition. Percy and George Murray were just 12 and 10 years old when these photographs were taken. They left behind not only a complete set of parents but also six siblings – all but one of whom eventually followed them to Canada. Ellinor Close, the woman who organised the scheme that took them to Canada, believed that she was helping them to a bright new future, but she also thought she was doing the right thing for her country, by removing weak, sickly children who would otherwise be a burden to the state, and sending them out to lead healthier and more useful lives in the colonies. Percy and George Murray may have experienced harsh conditions and psychological trauma by being taken to Canada at such a young age, but their experiences of life in a London workhouse were probably little better and both suffered from rickets. They and their

*Plate 5. The workhouse children (Plate 4) in Nauwigewerk, New Brunswick, Canada less than 6 months later. Not only were the children healthier, they were being kept at a fraction of the cost of maintaining them in England. George and Percy Murray were reunited with their family briefly during World War I when they came to Europe as soldiers in the Canadian Army. The height marker held by the woman in the back row is probably set at the same height in both pictures (5 feet) to emphasise just how short the children were for their age – even as an adult George Murray was only 5ft 4ins. (I am indebted to George's son, George Ernest, and to his great-niece, Jaqueline Murdoch for information about the Murray family.)
Source: LMA, 20.61 A-DUR*

descendants have prospered in a way that one suspects would not have been possible if they had remained in England. They certainly fared better than the one brother who stayed behind in England.

16. Further reading: the context of illegitimacy

Addy, J, *Sin and society in the seventeenth century* (Routledge, 1989).

Clark, A, *Working life of women in the seventeenth century* (London, 1919).

Emmison, F G, *Elizabethan life: morals and church courts* (Essex Record Office, 1973).

Fildes, V (ed), *Women as mothers in pre-industrial England* (Routledge, 1990).

Finlay, R, *Population and metropolis: the demography of London 1580-1650* (CUP, 1981).

Gillis, J, *For better, for worse: British marriages, 1600 to the present* (OUP, 1985).

Glass, D V and D E C Eversley (eds), *Population in history: essays in historical demography* (Edward Arnold, 1965).

Helmholz, R H, *Marriage litigation in medieval England* (CUP, 1974).

Helmholz, R H, 'Support orders, church courts, and the rule of *filius nullius*: a reassessment of the common law' and 'Bastardy litigation in medieval England' in *Canon Law and the law of England* (Hambledon Press, 1987).

Hill, B, *Women, work and sexual politics* (Blackwell, 1989).

Houlbrooke, R, *Church courts and the people during the English reformation 1520-1570* (OUP, 1979).

Houlbrooke, R, *The English family 1450-1700* (Longman, 1984).

Laslett, P, *The world we have lost* (Methuen, 1965).

Laslett, P, Oosterveen, and R M Smith (eds), *Bastardy and its comparative history* (Edward Arnold, 1980).

Macfarlane, A, *Marriage and love in England: modes of reproduction 1300-1840* (Blackwell, 1986).

Malcomson, R W, 'Infanticide in the eighteenth century' in J S Cockburn (ed), *Crime in England 1550-1800* (Methuen, 1977).

Menefee, S P, *Wives for sale: an ethnographic study of British popular divorce* (Blackwell, 1981).

Outhwaite, R B (ed), *Marriage and society: studies in the social history of marriage* (Europa, 1981).

Parker, S, *Informal marriage, cohabitation and the law, 1750-1989* (Macmillan, 1990)

Quaife, S, *Wanton wenches and wayward wives: peasants and illicit sex in early seventeenth-century England* (Croom Helm, 1979).

Reay, B (ed), *Popular culture in seventeenth century England* (Croom Helm, 1985).

Stone, L, *The family, sex and marriage in England 1500-1800,* (Weidenfeld and Nicolson, 1977).

Stone, L, *Road to divorce: England 1530-1987* (OUP, 1990).

Wrightson, K, *English society 1580-1680* (Hutchinson, 1982).

Wrigley, E A and R S Schofield, *The population history of England, 1541-1871: a reconstruction* (Edward Arnold, 1981).

PART II: PREPARING FOR A SEARCH

17. The preliminaries

The problem for us in trying to reconstruct social attitudes in the past is that their transmission was not uniform either by geographical area, social class or time period. The range of attitudes described here, from total and absolute disapproval of all pre-marital sex, to positive encouragement of pre-marital sex as long as any pregnancy led to marriage, co-existed in a complex pattern of overlapping priorities, prejudices and sheer pragmatism. Interpreting social attitudes was also a problem for our ancestors. It is not difficult to realise that social and geographical mobility would sometimes bring together young people whose cultural assumptions about pre-marital sexual behaviour did not match.

Stereotypically, we probably all find it easy to conjure up a picture of the abandoned girl 'seduced under promise of marriage' as her contemporaries so often described it. But it also happened the other way round. When a group of urban labourers were brought to Portland to build the new prison, they soon entered into relationships with local girls. Portland, as we have already seen, was one of those communities in which trial marriage was a commonly accepted part of courtship practices [4]. An outbreak of pregnancies soon demonstrated that the young men concerned had very different expectations to those of their host community: they had no intention of marrying and saw no reason to change their minds. Local outrage was vociferous – and violent. The expectant fathers rapidly came to an appreciation of the link between marriage and their continued physical safety: only one of the babies was born a bastard.

If our ancestors sometimes had difficulty in understanding the social rules that should have governed their lives, it is scarcely surprising that we find it difficult to do so, too. The only way that we can attempt it is by trying to locate the individuals in question geographically, socially and chronologically. Always be alert for the possibility that attempts to protect the unmarried mother and/or her child might lead to the recording of false or misleading information about them. This part of the guide will help you to devise a research strategy based on the case that you are trying to solve, but before you go any further, assemble what information you have and use it to answer three fundamental questions. When and where did your person live? What sort of area was it? What sort of social/occupational background did they have?

18. How can you be sure that your ancestor was a bastard?

It is sometimes easy to be misled. Do not assume too much too quickly. A marriage certificate issued after 1837 may show that the bride and groom were living at the same address. Yes, that could be because they were cohabiting. But it could also be that one or both were lodgers there or that they needed an accommodation address in order to marry in their favourite church or wanted to avoid the cost of having banns called in two parishes. If the name of the bride or bridegroom's father is missing from their marriage certificate it does not imply bastardy: it may simply reflect the quality of relationships in that family. Conversely do not assume that because a name *is* entered that it is the correct one: it could be an adoptive father, a stepfather, or a grandfather. It may even be totally fictitious. If you suspect bastardy, do not take any evidence at face value: someone, somewhere may have been covering up.

There is no substitute for getting back to the original birth record. From 1837 this is most likely to be a birth certificate, where the information given is closely constrained by legal requirements and where the absence of a father's name is fairly conclusive evidence of illegitimacy. However, there were few checks and in an urban area where neither the midwife nor the registrar knew all the residents, it would have been very easy for a single mother to invent an absent husband for the occasion. It is always worth looking a little more deeply into the information on the birth certificate. Who was the informant? If it was someone other than the mother it might be a valuable clue. Where was the birth? Do not be fooled into thinking that it is a private house just because the format of the address looks like one. It became a matter of policy not to identify institutions by name: births in St Pancras Workhouse took place at 4 Kings Road, St Pancras; those at Mile End Workhouse were registered as The Lodge, Bancroft Road. If the place of birth is somewhere other than the mother's normal residence then check it against a trade directory for the area [**43**].

Failure to trace a birth certificate, or a marriage certificate for the parents named on the birth certificate, could be the result of deliberately false information, and therefore indicative of illegitimacy. But again, do not jump to conclusions. As with any mass collection of data, the indexes to births, marriages and deaths maintained by the Office for National Statistics (formerly the General Register Office) inevitably contain errors. More importantly, they do not cover births, marriages or deaths that took place in Scotland, Ireland or the colonies. There are separate indexes for service personnel. Using sources such as census returns to check ages, relationships and places of birth for family members can be useful; but remember that the information they contain is only as good as the original informant who made it – like everyone else, your ancestors made mistakes, and sometimes they lied deliberately. Always be suspicious of the family with an unusually long age gap between siblings – maybe it really was like that, but maybe this is a family where an illegitimate child is being passed off as the child of its grandparents.

Baptismal registers [see **27**], being relatively unconstrained by legal requirements until 1813, vary considerably from parish to parish, and from period to period. It is unlikely that many men followed the example of the sixteenth century Lord Roos [**17**], who was so doubtful of the paternity of his wife's child that he insisted that the boy be called Ignotus (literally 'unknown'), but baptismal entries can nevertheless be informative. They need to be read very carefully. Some clearly identify illegitimate children but, as indicated below, you may need to learn a new vocabulary to interpret them [**Appendix 1**]. Do not be deceived into taking the entries at face value – the mother who is described as a whore, a harlot or a 'meretrix' (prostitute) may genuinely have been paid for sexual services, but is far more likely instead to have been a perfectly ordinary single mother. Sometimes entries are coded. Sometimes they are ambiguous, such as those where the child appears to have been given a different surname to that of its mother. These may indicate illegitimacy, but then again they may not. Do not jump to the conclusion that 'William, son of John Mitchell and Mary Somers' was necessarily a bastard. Perhaps he was, but he could just as easily have been the legitimate son of John Mitchell Somers and his wife Mary. You may be on safer ground assuming bastardy from an entry that clearly shows the child's surname to be different to that of its mother or that gives the name of the mother but omits the father altogether, but even then you will need to be careful; in the case of an entry for the baptism of 'John, son of widow Smith' for example you could be dealing with an illegitimate child born to a woman widowed many years before or with a legitimate but posthumous child.

Obviously, you will have to use baptismal registers for the period before civil registration was introduced in 1837, but do not ignore them for the period after that date. Although the introduction of pre-printed registers in 1813 meant that the information recorded became increasingly standardised, a few clergymen did continue to add idiosyncratic comments to their baptismal entries, some of which may identify the father or give you some much needed clues. This is particularly true of registers compiled specifically for workhouse use.

The other common pitfall for family history researchers is the use of an alias. Like the omission of the father's name on the marriage certificate or the ambiguous baptismal entry, it is all too easy to assume that John Davies alias Atkins used two surnames because his parents were not married. Of course, that could be the true explanation, but do not overlook the possibility that there are others, such as the adoption of the surname of a stepfather or the Anglicisation of a foreign surname (e.g. Schneider to Taylor).

Sometimes it is no more than a simple spelling variant. Saying the names out loud (especially if you can muster a regional accent) might help: Geoghan/Egan and St Clair/Sinclair/Sinkler do not look very alike on the page, but they are pronounced very similarly. It is quite likely that your ancestors were illiterate and that the spelling of their names reflects their pronunciation.

19. Getting started

There are certain pieces of knowledge that are fundamental and which will lay the foundations for a successful search.

You will almost always need to find the original birth record. This can be surprisingly difficult, especially in cases of informal adoption before 1927, when the birth name may not be known. Remember that under the English common law your legal name is the one by which you are generally known. The names given in the records of births and marriages may not indicate a change of name. If a person adopted the surname of a stepfather or that of the family who brought him up or used the name of a birth father when the birth record used the mother's name only, then it will be difficult, perhaps impossible, to link him to his own birth record. Information from census entries may help by pinpointing the place of birth.

- If your person was born in a mother and baby hostel, was adopted or spent time in a children's home, then try to trace the records of the society concerned just in case they include a personal file with valuable information about family background.
- Collect as many family legends and memories as you can in the hope that buried amongst them will be a vital clue, perhaps including a birth name or information about a birth family. Review what you have learned in the light of some of the legal and cultural factors that have been described in Part I. The sort of family story that ends with the phrase 'It was a good thing there was a will' may well be indicative of the *'filius nullius'* rule or of an informal adoption – especially if you are looking at a relatively poor family who would not normally be expected to bother about one.
- Check to see whether anyone in the family (not just the mother) left a will. Wills are always useful for family historians; in the case of illegitimate children, or of children adopted before 1927, they are invaluable since they provided the easiest mechanism by which blood or adoptive relatives could ensure the appropriate transmission of property rights.

- If the time span is appropriate, check the family on successive censuses: information about ages, relationships, birthplace and the neighbourhood in which they lived could all provide useful clues for further research.
- Check to see whether the mother married after the birth, and check too for the birth of siblings. This may be enough to establish whether or not the mother was in a stable relationship. It will also give you additional information and dates that can be followed into other sets of records.
- Look closely at family naming patterns. Does your illegitimate ancestor have a middle name when most of the rest of the family have only one forename? Do any of the forenames resemble a surname? This could be a clue to a paternal surname. Like all clues it needs to be treated with care: it could just as easily be a tribute to a godparent or other benefactor.
- Take advantage of research that others have already done. There may already be some published work on the family that interests you. Check out the works listed in [45] by Marshall, Thomson and Whitmore. There is a good collection of unpublished material at the library of the Society of Genealogists. Explore published and unpublished research on patterns of marriage and fertility in the particular period, parish or region that interests you. The advice of the local studies librarian and local archivists will be invaluable – but their task will obviously be made much easier if you can do a certain amount of preparatory searching yourself, perhaps in one of the many catalogues now available on the internet, such as that of the British Library and the Library of Congress. Unpublished research theses submitted for higher degrees at British universities can be located via the History online database maintained at the Institute of Historical Research. The Royal Historical Society provides a specialist online database of history publications. [46]
- Link up with others. The Guild of One Name Studies publishes its register annually and also maintains a website with details of its members' societies. There are also a number of published registers of surname interests, such as Johnson and Sainty's *Genealogical Research Directory* and the *British Isles genealogical register* or *BIG-R*. Local family history societies publish lists of members' interests. If you are lucky you may also find that they have published indexes and transcripts of local records. Even if they have not they will offer a forum for mutual support that you may find invaluable in itself. Online links to lists of UK surnames being researched together with other useful information for those researching family history in the British Isles are available over the internet from GENUKI.

20. Devising a search strategy

The range of sources that might be useful is so vast and the quality of information that they give so variable that it is almost impossible to advise on a search strategy without knowing the individual circumstances of each case. However the simplified search plan [**Appendix 2**] and the following tips should help you to decide where to start looking.

If the person you are seeking was born after 1844 into a relatively poor family, then the most obvious first step is to look for a maintenance (affiliation) order [see **24**]. Because the survival of such records is often poor, you should also explore the records of the local Board of Guardians [see **40**] especially if your check on the address given as the place of birth on the birth certificate establishes that it was a workhouse. If your person is known to have been in an institution then look for its records [see **42**]. Finding out something about the institution will always be useful. If nothing else it will help you understand some of the influences that shaped his/her life. It may give you extra clues to follow. Equally it may help to establish that some avenues of research are not worth following. If, for example, the fees charged by the institution were higher than the sum normally awarded to the mother under a maintenance order then you can probably assume:

•   that poor law records are not worth searching because the Board of Guardians would look for somewhere cheaper;
•   that irrespective of the title of the organisation, it was not catering for destitute children, and that there was probably some kind of voluntary agreement with the father [**41**].

The restrictions imposed by the 1834 Poor Law Amendment Act [**12**] probably make the decade between 1834 and 1844 one of the most difficult in which to conduct a successful search for further information about illegitimate births. Where the family is known to be poor, it is essential to check poor law records [**40**] and as with the period after 1844 you should also look for the records of any institution in which the child is known to have lived [**42**]. It may also be worth looking at published materials since there was enormous opposition to the new system, resulting in the publication of pamphlets and newspaper articles about cases of hardship [**37**]. Again private papers may be useful for tracking down voluntary agreements [**41**].

If you are researching a person born between 1531 and 1834, then start with the records of the old poor law [**39**]. Because the system was designed to prevent an illegitimate child from becoming chargeable the documentation it created reached up to a higher level of society than after 1834, but it will still exclude the affluent who are more likely to have made private agreements [**41**].

For those born before 1640, you should also check any surviving records of the church and manorial courts [**30**; **36**].

If the person you are seeking were born into a reasonably affluent family (or had an affluent father) then you may find that the search becomes extremely difficult. As indicated above [**19**] looking for wills will be crucial. If you are lucky the family itself may have left a cache of personal papers, or you may be able to identify the family's solicitor and find further documentation that way [**41**]. Realistically, however, you need to be prepared for the possibility that your search is likely to involve piecing together multiple fragments of information that might lead you into published sources [**37**], prosecutions [**30**], records of disputes [**31**] or divorce [*see* **32**], any or all of which might help solve your problem (or just as easily turn out to be dead ends).

21. Reading the records

It can be difficult to read nineteenth- and twentieth-century records. This is either a straightforward issue of bad handwriting, or it is about the quality of materials that our ancestors used to record information – flimsy, acidic paper, blotchy pens or (as users of early census returns will know to their cost) faint pencils. Earlier records are quite different. Although they are written, by and large, by people who took pride in their literacy and who formed their letters carefully and regularly, the letter shapes they used were quite different to the ones we use now. If your research is going to take you into records written before about 1700, then you will need to learn how to read at least some of these older scripts. You will also need to be aware that although the records of the equity courts, and those that used similar procedures (Star Chamber and the Court of Requests) were in English and in the common hand of the day, until 1733 (apart from a brief period in the mid seventeenth century) the formal records of most courts (writs, summonses and indictments) were written not only in special legal scripts but also in heavily abbreviated Latin.

Don't give up! It is not as difficult as you think. There are a number of very good guides to old handwriting (palaeography), and to the kind of formulaic Latin that is present in the most commonly used family history documents. Some are listed below [**45**] and should be available to borrow via the library service or to buy from family history societies and the Society of Genealogists. It is also worth asking about adult education services in your area: there are lots of courses available, some specifically designed for family historians, including those at the Society of Genealogists. There are even courses on the internet. [**46**]

PART III: FINDING AND USING THE SOURCES

22. Archives and libraries in England and Wales

The most comprehensive guide to archives in England and Wales is by Foster and Shepherd [**45**]. However this is a fairly substantial tome normally only found in libraries and record offices; the guide by Gibson and Peskett [**45**] is more likely to fit your pocket (physically as well as financially). You can also find out details of addresses and opening hours of most archives through the internet site of the Royal Commission on Historical Manuscripts, now part of The National Archives [**46**]. This site will also guide you to the National Register of Archives and a database of archive holdings in the UK.

Many archives, including The National Archives, now have online browsable catalogues, and an increasing number of them can be searched through A2A (the Access to Archives project) which is available through The National Archives website. Online catalogues can be immensely useful but also deceptive. Most archives have built up their lists over several decades; in many cases they are still using the finding aids designed by the clerks who filed the documents when they were created. So bear in mind that a catalogue is simply an overall description of the holdings, it is not a detailed index to the names (or places) that appear in the records. There will almost certainly be other, and possibly more useful, indexes at the archive office itself. Make sure that you explore the website fully: it probably contains a lot of useful advice about using the collections, perhaps including specialised leaflets for family history use.

Information about family history resources in public libraries in Britain and Ireland can be searched at *Familia*, the internet family history portal hosted by Co-East, a consortium of public library authorities.

Plan your research visit carefully. Make sure that you check opening hours and holdings before you go. Allow sufficient time to familiarise yourself with the way the catalogues and indexes work. Find out whether an appointment is needed and what identification you will require. If you take notes by hand you will need pencils; if you use a laptop computer, check whether a socket will be available.

23. Adoption

Before 1927
[See: **40; 41; 42**].

After 1927

The original intention of legalising adoption was to make a complete break between the child and his/her natural parents. Accordingly it was not possible for either the adopted child or the birth parent to trace the link between the adoption certificate and the original birth record. This changed in 1975, when it became possible for adopted persons to have access to their birth record. Those adopted before 11 November 1975 are required to see an adoption counsellor before being given the information to enable them to apply for a certificate from their birth entry. This information includes a person's original name, the mother's name and the registration district in which the birth took place. The counsellor will also supply an authorisation that will enable the court that made the adoption order to release the name of the adoption society or local authority (if any) that arranged the adoption. Free leaflets on adoption issues are available from the General Register Office or its website [See also: **47**; **46**].

It is important, however, to realise that there can be no guarantee that the court's records survive, let alone those of an adoption society or of a local authority. A lot of small children's organisations may no longer exist. Of those that do survive, many may not have thought it necessary to retain detailed files once the children concerned had reached adulthood. Nor should you be surprised to discover that one or both of the adoptive parents were also birth parents. [See also: **39; 40; 41**].

24. Affiliation orders (after 1844)

In order to trace affiliation orders after 1844, you need to know the mother's address at the time of the application so that you can identify the petty sessional court responsible for hearing the case. This is likely to be the nearest court, but you may need to seek advice at the relevant record office about the boundaries of local petty sessional divisions. Petty sessional records are usually held at local record offices.

The original process would have involved an application for a summons against the alleged father, a record that a summons was issued and an adjudication. The documents are likely to be filed by type rather than by case, and to consist of standard (probably pre-printed) forms that are filed by date, often in bound volumes. It is most unlikely that they will be indexed by name. If you are lucky, all the documents may have survived, but since the information they contain tends to overlap, then simply finding one may be sufficient.

Applications for a summons may be filed in two series: those made before the birth and those made after the birth. Both will give the date of the complaint, name and address of the mother, the name and address (sometimes including occupation) of the alleged father and the signature of the mother. Those made after the birth additionally give details of the date and place of the child's birth. Some of the documents may be annotated with useful additional information such as the date of the summons and hearing. The orders themselves give the date of the hearing, the name and address of the mother, the name and address of the father, the date and place of birth of the child and details of the payments to be made. Later annotations sometimes give information about the service of the order on the father, perhaps revealing a new address for him, or details of an application to change or revoke it on the grounds that the parties have now married each other. Occasionally the mother's name is given in a form that enables you to infer that the couple have been in a stable union and were passing themselves off as man and wife.

Unfortunately, records of petty sessions courts often do not survive well until the later nineteenth century, and discrete series of bastardy applications and orders such as those described above may not survive until the early years of the twentieth century. If petty sessional records survive, but do not appear to include bastardy records for the right dates, do not give up without investigating further. Daily minute books and/or registers of summons issued, could give you most of the information you need. Minute books may (with luck) contain a very full record of the evidence heard, and can be very revealing about the social attitudes of the time. They are likely to be handwritten and

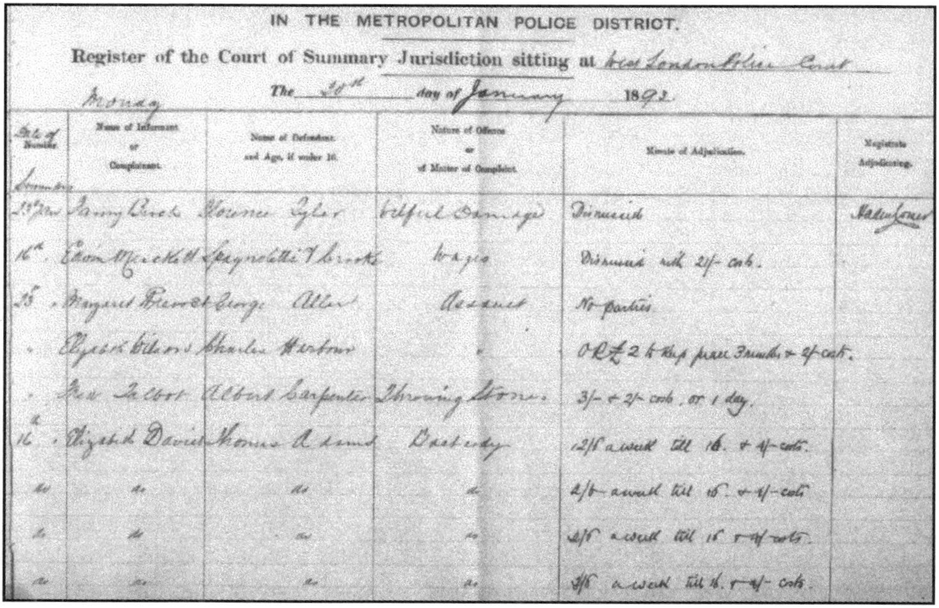

Plate 6. Petty sessions register 1893. In the absence of other surviving records, the registers of summons can supply limited but still useful information. Source: LMA, PS.WLN/A2/20 Crown Copyright

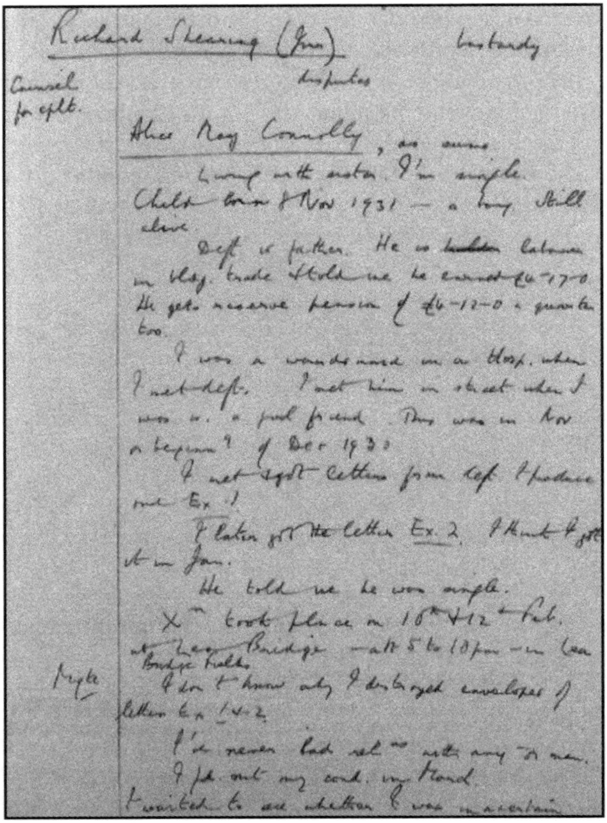

Plate 7. Petty sessions minutes, 1931. Unindexed and difficult to read - but notes like these, probably scribbled down whilst the parties were giving their evidence, provide a wonderful insight into the lives of our ancestors. Source: LMA, PS/CLE/B06/02, p. 22. Crown Copyright

arranged chronologically, but are unlikely to be indexed by either name or place. Registers of summons issued are far less rich. They will probably contain standard forms, often pre-printed and they will be arranged by date with no name indexes. They give the date of summons, the name of the informant/complainant, the name of the defendant and his/her age if under 16, the nature of the offence/complaint, a note of the adjudication and the name of the adjudicating magistrate. You may hit the jackpot and find evidence of a long but broken relationship: in 1893, for example, Londoner Elizabeth Davies applied for not one but four summonses against her erstwhile lover, Thomas Adams. She was awarded 2s. 6d. (12.5p) a week and 4s. (20p) costs on each count. The drawback is that such entries rarely name the child or children and do not give addresses or ages, so with a common name it can be difficult to be sure that you have found the right entry. Applications for summonses against fathers alleging bastardy or for arrears on an existing bastardy order will be mixed up with all sorts of petty offences such as failure to attend school, cruelty to horses, obstruction and assault, but they are quite easy to pick out. You will probably be able to scan through a register of summonses far more quickly than a minute book, so if both survive use the register to find the date of the hearing and then move to the minute book for fuller details.

If there are no petty sessional records at all, do not despair. Look for newspaper reports of petty sessions hearings. Check poor law records [40]; if the birth was in the period 1844-1858 check bastardy returns [26].

25. Apprenticeship records

The best source of information about the apprenticing of pauper bastard children, if it survives at all, will be amongst the records of the parish (vestry papers) that apprenticed them – their parish of settlement. These will normally be in the local record office. You will need to check accounts, minutes, registers of apprentices and apprenticeship indentures, none of which are likely to be indexed by name. Some or all of these may include additional information about paternity. Remember that a bastard was settled in the parish of birth. If you do not know the parish of birth, you will need to find it. The section on birth records [27] may help. Bear in mind that an application for poor relief later in life may reveal details of the apprenticeship, so check records for the area(s) in which your person lived as an adult [*see* 39; 40]. If the child concerned was cared for by a charitable foundation or rescue home then also check their records for information about apprenticeships: the Foundling Hospital, for example, kept its own apprenticeship registers [42].

A commonly used source for apprenticeships between 1710 and 1811 is held at the Public Record Office. This consists of registers compiled for tax purposes. *These will not help you trace pauper apprentices*: parishes and charitable institutions were exempt from the tax.

26. Bastardy returns, 1844-1858

Bastardy returns were required from each petty sessions, 1844-1858, and had to give the name of the mother, the date of the summons, the date of the hearing, the result of the application, and the name of the father. The various clerks of petty sessions managed to interpret these requirements very differently. The clerk at Kensington petty sessions regularly included a complete summary of the proceedings, the addresses of the alleged fathers (some from as far away as Glasgow), and often their occupations, too. On one occasion he even added the father's warrant number (he was a police constable). Even more unusually, he also recorded the names of alleged fathers even if the case against them had been dismissed. Other clerks were far less diligent and included as little information as was necessary to comply with the law.

Annual lists of appeals to quarter sessions were also compiled, 1844-1858. These give the name of the appellant (the alleged father), the name of the mother, the name of the petty sessions where the order was made, the result of the appeal and sometimes also give details of costs awarded. Clerks of the peace were supposed to forward copies to the Home Office.

Surviving lists of appeals and bastardy returns are most likely to be found in the local record office, amongst the records of quarter sessions. At the London Metropolitan Archives, however, Middlesex returns are held in a separate series relating to summary jurisdiction. These records are not well known either to family historians or to archivists; you may have to search the catalogues very carefully in order to verify their existence. No such lists are known to survive amongst the records of the Home Office (which are held in the Public Record Office now known as The National Archives).

27. Birth, marriages and deaths before 1837

Church of England parish registers
Thomas Cromwell ordered the keeping of parish registers in 1538. In 1597 another order went out requiring existing registers to be copied into 'fair parchment books'. Although some of the pre-1597 paper books do still exist, for many parishes the 1597 copies are the earliest surviving records. Note that in this context the 'parish' is a parish of the Anglican Church (also known as Church of England and in the USA as Episcopalian). Most people in England and Wales were members of this church.

Parish registers do not always survive, but those that do are usually held in the local record office; many early parish registers have been published. The *National Index to Parish Registers* which will tell you what registers have survived, where they are held and whether there are transcripts or indexes available. A list of holdings in the library of the Society of Genealogists is available via their website [**46**]. Even if the actual parish registers no longer exist, it is possible that some of the information in them does survive in the form of Bishops' Transcripts. These are contemporary records made, as the name suggests, for the bishop of the diocese. They often omit important details – especially for illegitimate children. Conversely they may include information that was not recorded in the parish register. Surviving Bishops' Transcripts are held in diocesan record offices: use Gibson, *Bishops' Transcripts* and the *National Index to Parish Registers* to locate them [**45**].

The format of the early registers varies considerably. Some parishes kept separate books for baptisms, marriages and burials; some did not. Some registers are terse; some are eloquent. Before 1813, there were virtually no regulations governing the entries of baptisms: you can always expect to find the date of baptism, the name of the child and

Plate 8. Return of bastardy appeals, Middlesex, 1844. Between 1844 and 1858, each county in England and Wales had to make annual returns of appeals like this. Source: LMA, MSJ/RB/19/2 Crown Copyright

Appellant	Respondent	When Order made	Result of appeal
Henry Stephens	Elizabeth Hall	Bow Street Police Court	Order confirmed Costs £2
Thomas Powell	Elizabeth Hall	Kensington Petty Session	Order confirmed
Richard Gardner	Jane Hall	Marylebone police Court	Appeal disallowed
James Edmund Style	Eliza Margaret Whitting	Clerkenwell police court	Order quashed
George Turner	Mary Gorman	Hammersmith police court	Order confirmed costs £6.4.6
John Flower	Jane Harris	Clerkenwell police court	Order confirmed costs £1.10.0
James Brown	Esther Sophia Hyams	ditto	Order confirmed cost £3.3.0
Edward Wm Saunders	Rosina Allen Hill	Worship Street police court	Order confirmed Costs £10
William Thomas	Emma Smith	Edmonton Petty Session	Appeal dismissed

1844.

County of Middlesex — Division of Uxbridge

Name of Mother of Bastard applying	Date of Issue of Summons	Date of Petty Sessions	Result of the Application	Names of the putative Father and cases in which returned
Mary Treadaway	9th Sept 1844	23 September 1844	Abandoned	
Fanny Stow	16 September	30th September	Order made 2/ per week and costs	James Giles
Eliza Mercer	21st October	4 November	Abandoned	
Elizabeth Allen	28th October	11 November	Abandoned	
Mary Milton	11 November	25th November	Order made 2/ per week and costs	William Burton
Caroline Parker	18th November	2nd December	Order made 5/ per week for the first six weeks & 2/6 afterwards and costs	John Rogers
Eliza Gregory	2nd December	16th December	Order refused	

We certify the above list to be correct in all particulars

Plate 9. Bastardy return, Uxbridge petty sessions, 1844. Between 1844 and 1858, each petty sessions court had to make an annual return of bastardy cases. This return contains sufficient information to comply with the new law and no more; other petty sessions returns are sometimes rather more informative. Source: LMA, MSJ/RB/16/1 Crown Copyright (usually) the name of the father; from the seventeenth century they will usually contain the names of both parents, and sometimes the occupation of the father is also given. Often they will add snippets of extra detail indicating, for example, that the child is a twin or triplet, or giving the actual date of birth. Some parishes kept separate registers of baptisms of the illegitimate. Illegitimacy may be indicated in the entry in a number of ways – researchers have identified over 80 different words and phrases used to indicate bastardy [**Appendix 1**]. Illegitimacy can also be indicated by describing the mother as a harlot or similarly pejorative description.

From 1813 baptismal registers were normally recorded on pre-printed forms bound into registers and give the date of baptism, the name of the child, and the names and residence of its parents, as well as the occupation of the father. The term 'residence' is a somewhat loose one – it could be as precise as a street or a farm, or as imprecise as a village. Some clergymen still managed to add interesting details and comments. Parish registers rarely give the mother's maiden name.

Marriage registers were kept more meticulously from 1754 as a result of Hardwicke's Marriage Act. They give the names and parish of the bride and groom, the date of the ceremony and whether it was by banns or licence. They often also give marital status and occasionally the groom's occupation. The entries are authenticated by the signatures or marks of the couple, the clergyman and at least two witnesses. Since the act also required the calling of banns, these were also recorded often in the register itself or in a separate banns register, but sometimes on loose sheets of paper. From 1824 banns had to be kept in a register. The banns recorded in this way may not result in an entry in the marriage register, either because the marriage took place in another parish or because it did not take place at all. They can occasionally be extremely revealing. Records of licences to marry can be traced using Gibson, *Bishops' Transcripts and Marriage Licences* [**45**].

Burial registers regularly give the date of the burial and the name of the deceased. From 1812 they usually give the age at death, and some earlier registers also may also record this. If you are exceptionally lucky, the register may also give you the cause of death, place of residence, and some information about family relationships.

Non-parochial records

The term nonconformist or dissenter is normally used to describe members of protestant sects other than Anglicans. The main groups were Baptists, Congregationalists, Independents, Methodists, Presbyterians, and Quakers. Some of these groups used Anglican churches for burials (since they often had no burial ground of their own) and, in conformity with Hardwicke's Marriage Act, for marriages, so entries for these events are often found in the Anglican parish registers. Such congregations also kept their own records, including baptismal registers. Most nonconformist registers were handed in to the new Registrar General either shortly after the introduction of civil registration in 1837 or in 1857. Registers from some Catholic and foreign churches together with some non-parochial Anglican registers were also handed in. These registers are available on microfilm at The National Archives and online through the BMD Registers website [47]. Copies of the films are also held by LDS family history centres and by many local record offices and libraries. Nonconformist registers that have been completed since that time are normally held in the local record office.

The National Archives also hold copies of records and registers of the Society of Friends (Quakers) for the period 1613-1841, as well as the registers compiled by the Protestant Dissenters' Registry, 1742-1837 (Dr Williams' Library) and by the Wesleyan Methodist Metropolitan Registry, 1813-1838).

The National Archives' holdings of non-parochial registers are described more fully by Bevan and Shorney [45]. In searching for illegitimate ancestors it is probably worth spreading the search into a wider range of nonconformist records since the congregations often also acted to punish their members for moral transgressions by suspending them from membership or imposing some other shaming punishment. Use the *National Index to Parish Registers* and the *My Ancestors Were* ... guides by Breed, Clifford, Leary and Ruston listed in the bibliography below [45] to locate them.

[*See* also: **34**]

28. Births, marriages and deaths after 1837

Civil registration
Civil registration in England and Wales began in July 1837. From 1983 there are annual indexes; before that date the indexes are quarterly. Remember that the quarterly indexes are based on the date of registration rather than that of the event. In cases of birth, for example, parents had up to six weeks to register, so occasionally a birth will appear to be in the 'wrong' quarter – a birth in December 1867 may not have been registered until the following January and will therefore appear in the index for the quarter ending March 1868. Microfiche copies of the indexes up to the present day are available for public consultation free of charge at several libraries addresses of which can be found via the General Register Office website. Microfiche copies for various other earlier dates are also available at LDS family history centres and in many libraries and record offices, where they are often known as 'St Catherine's House indexes'. Birth, marriage and death indexes are also available online through several commercial websites and the free FreeBMD website.

Births

The birth indexes are alphabetical by surname, and also give the child's forename(s) and the district in which (s)he was registered. From the September quarter of 1911 they also give the maiden surname of the mother. Foundlings are indexed at the end of the alphabetical sequence until 1977 when they are inserted under the surname that was allocated to them. Registration of births was easily evaded until 1875 and stillbirths were not registered at all until 1 July 1927. Stillbirths do not appear in the indexes (see under Deaths, below).

The information given in the indexes may not be enough to identify the correct certificate, especially if the surname is particularly common. If you end up unable to choose between several different index entries but have some additional information (e.g. names of parents, or date or place of birth) you can use the reference checking service which allows you to list all the index entries and to specify that you want only the one that conforms to your additional information. There is a charge for each check undertaken, but it is cheaper than having to pay for a wrong certificate.

Birth certificates normally contain the following information: the date and place of birth, the name and sex of the child, the name and occupation of the father, the name and former surname(s) of the mother, the name, address and status of the person registering the birth (usually a parent). The 1837 Act of Parliament that introduced civil registration specified 'that it shall not be necessary to register the name of any father of a bastard child'. In the absence of clear instructions, some registrars entered the father's name even if the couple were not married and the father was not present at the registration; others did not allow the father's details to be entered at all. By 1850 the legal requirements had been clarified and registrars were instructed that a putative father could not be named, even if he was willing to sign the entry as informant.

The Registration Act of 1875 stated that 'The putative father of an illegitimate child cannot be required as father to give information respecting the birth. The name, surname and occupation of the putative father of an illegitimate child must not be entered except at the joint request of the father and mother; in which case both the father and mother must sign the entry as informants'. If the names of both parents are given as the informants in column 7 after 1875, then you should assume that they were not married to each other at the time of the birth of the child.

Marriages

Until the end of 1911 the marriage indexes are alphabetical by surname and also give the forename(s) of each person marrying together with the name of the registration district in which the marriage was solemnised. If you know the names of both parties then you can check that you have the right entry by matching the two index entries to each other. From the March quarter of 1912, each index entry also contains the surname of the spouse.

The marriage certificate will give the date of the marriage, the name of the place of worship or register office, whether it was by banns, notice or licence, the names of the bride and bridegroom, their ages, marital status (bachelor/spinster, widower or divorced), their occupations and addresses. It will also indicate whether they were literate enough to sign the register, the name of the person who performed the ceremony and the names of two or more witnesses. It normally also includes the names and occupations of the fathers of the bride and groom.

Note the denomination of the place of worship. If it is described as the 'parish church' or if the ceremony is said to be 'according to the rites and ceremonies of the established church' then the marriage was conducted in a church belonging to the Church of England. If the place of marriage belonged to any other religious denomination then this will be explicitly stated. If you need to track back into church records then this kind of information about the family's religious affiliation will be essential.

Deaths

The death indexes are alphabetical by the surname of the deceased and also give their forename(s) and the name of the registration district in which the death occurred. From the March quarter of 1866 the index entries also include the age at death; from 1969 the date of birth (often an estimate) is given instead of the age at death.

The certificates give name, sex and address of the deceased, age (as given by informant) and place of death. It also includes information about occupation, cause of death (and should indicate whether an inquest was held), as well as the name of the informant. As noted above, the death indexes do not include stillbirths; certified copies of records of stillbirths cannot be obtained without the consent of the Registrar General.

Obtaining the certificates

It is important for searchers to realise that the name of the registration district may not be the same as the name of the parish or village in which the event took place. If you are not familiar with the geography of the area concerned then you may find it useful to consult a guide to registration districts such as that by Wiggins [*see* **45**].

Once you have identified a likely entry, you will need to note the details in order to buy the certificate. You can apply for a certificate by post or online from the General Registry Office, but the certificate itself will be prepared at the headquarters of the registration service in Southport and will be posted to you. If you cannot apply in person then you will need to make an application by telephone, e-mail or post [**46; 47**].

If you are unable to get access to the indexes, it is still possible to make an application for a certificate, but it will cost more. Current fees and details of how to apply are available from the website of the General Register Office [46].

[*See* also: 34]

29. Census records

Censuses have been taken in England and Wales at ten year intervals since 1801. The earliest were simply head counts; but a few original returns do survive in local record offices; use Gibson and Medlycott or Chapman to locate them [45]. Detailed returns containing personal information about individuals survive for the censuses of 1841, 1851, 1861, 1871, 1881, 1891 and 1901; all are available on microfilm (or microfiche) at The National Archives. Copies of the films are also available through LDS family history centres. Most local record offices have copies of the films for their areas; check their holdings by using Gibson and Hampson, *Census Returns on Microform* [45]. Census records were collected under a confidentiality promise so they are closed for 100 years. The 1841-1911 Censuses are also available online [46]. Some counties are also available on CD-ROM both for 1901 and earlier.

The information contained in the returns varies from census to census. Each gives full name, age, gender, and occupation. In the 1841 census exact ages were given for those under 15, but the ages of older people were rounded down to the nearest five years; in later censuses the age was supposed to be exact for everyone. From 1851 the full address was given together with marital status, relationship to head of household, and parish and county of birth. All census records are arranged by address rather than by name, so it could be difficult to trace particular individuals without an index. All available censuses are now indexed online through various commercial websites usually accessible through local libraries and record offices. For further guidance on identifying and using census records see Briant Rosier, Higgs and Lumas [45].

30. Criminal prosecutions

Immorality
Single mothers (and their partners) could be prosecuted in a number of courts. The church courts and, from the seventeenth century, the magistrates in quarter sessions played a major role in policing immorality. Do not be misled by some of the wording used in the church court records: a charge of adultery does not necessarily mean that the person concerned was actually married; it was often used as just another word for sinful sex. Prosecutions for immorality in the church courts may be classified as 'office cases' or may have been heard summarily during a Bishop's visitation. Where records survive, there is a good chance that they will provide a wealth of information about the nature and quality of people's personal relationships. Church court records are particularly informative as the process relied on written rather than verbal evidence, but the resulting documents are likely to be filed in several, complex and interlinking series that are extremely difficult to use. Neither church nor quarter sessions records are likely to be systematically indexed by name.

Brawls and duels
If you have reason to believe that your ancestors became involved in some kind of fight about the circumstances surrounding an illegitimate pregnancy then it may be worth searching for records of a prosecution. Be warned, however, firstly, that the trial records may not be very informative and, secondly, that until at least the late nineteenth century prosecutions were brought privately and that the prosecutor was free to choose the most appropriate court for his purpose. Assault could be prosecuted at almost any level of the judicial system. It could be tried by a single justice sitting in summary jurisdiction, at petty sessions (two or more justices in summary jurisdiction), as a full jury trial at quarter sessions, or perhaps even assizes. Some assaults were tried in Star Chamber or the King's Bench (Crown Side) which were the highest criminal courts in the country. Unless you have a good source of information that provides some clues about which court to try first, then your search will be lengthy and potentially unrewarding.

Duelling is a rather different matter. Despite all that you may read about the duelling code of honour, it was not at all unusual for a man to be prosecuted for challenging another to a duel. Records of these trials are likely to be in the records of the King's Bench (Crown Side), but it will be easier to search press reports.

Felonies: bigamy, rape and unlawful killing
Bigamy was an offence against church law, and from 1603 it was also a serious criminal offence. Trials for bigamy before 1603 are therefore most likely to be found in the records of the church courts and should be traced in the same way as those for

immorality. Criminal trials after 1603 were conducted at assizes or courts with equivalent jurisdiction such as the Old Bailey.

Prosecutions arising from rape and unlawful deaths, whether from a duel, infanticide, the neglect or abuse of a child, or at the hands of an illegal abortionist would normally have been heard at the local assize court or, in the London area, at the Old Bailey. See also [33]. Given the difficulty of securing a conviction for rape, however, many women preferred to prosecute for attempted rather than actual rape. These prosecutions are more likely to have been tried at quarter sessions. In the medieval period prosecutions for abortion and infanticide were occasionally heard in the church courts.

Locating the records
Records of the church courts are held in diocesan record offices which are usually, but not always, combined with local record offices. To locate them use Owen; for advice on their arrangement and contents use Tarver and Chapman [45]. Many records of Bishops' Visitations have been published, so make sure that you check what is available for your area.

Surviving records of summary jurisdiction and of quarter sessions are in local record offices. Records of justices acting alone or at petty sessions survive poorly until at least the late nineteenth century. For details of survival and coverage of quarter sessions records use Gibson, *Quarter Sessions Records* [45].

Records of trials for Middlesex (which covered most of modern London) held at the Old Bailey before 1834 are held at London Metropolitan Archives, and records of trials for the City of London held at the Old Bailey before 1834 are held at London's Guildhall. Records of the Old Bailey (renamed the Central Criminal Court) after 1834, of assize courts and of the King's Bench (Crown Side) are all in The National Archives. For further details see Bevan [45].

Using trial records
Although some criminal trial records have been published, for example in the *Calendar of Assize Records* which covers the counties of Essex, Hertfordshire, Kent, Surrey and Sussex for the sixteenth and seventeenth centuries, there are no national indexes to criminal records. Trial records are very formal and are full of legal fictions that can be very misleading to those who are not familiar with them. Until 1733 the formal records are in heavily abbreviated Latin and in distinctive legal scripts. The records are unlikely to include useful family history information or any transcript of the evidence given in court. Note also that assize records after about 1830 have been heavily weeded. You may find it both easier and ultimately more informative to look for a newspaper or pamphlet account of the trial. The most famous series of trial pamphlets

is known as the Old Bailey Sessions Papers. It gives very full accounts of trials at the Old Bailey. Copies for the period 1674 to 1834 are gradually being made available on the internet, and are fully searchable [46]. Fuller advice on the content and coverage of records of trials and convicted prisoners, the common pitfalls of using them and advice on further reading is given in Bevan; you might also find it useful to consult Hawkings and Paley [45].

[See also: 33; 37; 38]

31. Disputes: the records of the superior courts

The records of the superior courts are held in The National Archives. They administered two different forms of justice. Common law, which was used by the courts of King's Bench and Common Pleas, was based on the common customs of the country. The courts of Chancery and Exchequer both had a small common law jurisdiction but mainly used a system known as equity, which empowered the judges to give verdicts according to conscience and justice. Both systems had advantages and disadvantages for the user. The common law courts, for example, could award damages for breach of contract but the courts of equity could not. Conversely, the equity courts could order one of the parties to carry out the terms of a contract, but could not award damages for failure to do so. A litigant's success thus depended as much on choosing the correct court and remedy as on the facts of the case being litigated. In 1875 the old courts were abolished and a single High Court of Judicature was created in their place.

Some general comments on the records follow, but for more detailed advice see Bevan [45]. You should note from the outset that these records are extremely difficult to use and that the finding aids are generally inadequate. A speculative search could pay off handsomely but it will be both frustrating and extremely time consuming. It is almost certainly better to approach this kind of search via published material [*see* 35; 37].

Disputes about property
Many disputes about property, including allegations that certain individuals were debarred from inheritance by illegitimacy and problems resulting from divorce or separations, were heard in the equity courts. The records are in English and provide an unrivalled window on family life. The catch is that they are filed in several separate series which makes it difficult to re-assemble all the relevant parts of a single case. Searches are becoming easier with the advent of The National Archives' electronic catalogue and a parallel project to put the existing indexes into a database known as the Equity Pleadings Database. In the meantime you may need to start with the Bernau Index which is available on microfilm at the Society of Genealogists and at LDS family history centres. The Bernau Index is far from perfect. It gives obsolete

references, makes no attempt to standardise surname variants and rarely gives any additional information that would allow the user to distinguish between individuals bearing the same name. When using it make sure that you copy down the whole of the reference that is given – because you are going to need all that information in order to translate it into a modern reference to use at The National Archives. Use Sharp or Lawton to translate your references. There are also good general guides to using equity records by Horwitz, Gerhold and Trowles [45]. Leaflets on The National Archives website [46] will help you identify the best way to start your search.

Suits for breach of promise/loss of services before 1875
Until 1875, actions of this sort had to be commenced in the central common law courts at Westminster, although in practice many were actually heard locally at the assize courts under a system known as *nisi prius*. Such actions are extremely difficult to trace because there are no central indexes and there were several courts with overlapping jurisdictions. The records are complex, badly listed and imperfectly understood, even by experts. Furthermore much of the documentation that would bring a case to life has been weeded out. Unless you have picked up a clue from some other source, you will simply not know where to start. Even if you do know where to start, the use of Latin before 1733, and of legal fictions and formulae may mean that you will not fully understand the very formal records that do survive. It is almost certainly going to be easier to search through published material first to see if there is a printed reference to the case. Our ancestors were just as interested as we are in reading about cases of sex and seduction, so there is a good chance that this kind of approach will pay off [*see* 35; 37].

Actions in the superior courts after 1875
After 1875 the courts were reorganised into a single Supreme Court of Judicature. The reorganisation meant that legal business was allocated along functional lines by type and could be treated according to the principles of common law or rules of equity, whichever seemed most appropriate. Actions for breach of promise or loss of service are likely to have been heard by the division known (depending on the sex of the reigning monarch) as either the King's or Queen's Bench Division, and disputes about land by the Chancery Division. Records are filed by type rather than by case so it is difficult to trace all the surviving material for any one case. If you still want to try, make sure that you read the case study on using the records, by Watts and Watts [45].

32. Divorce

Before 1858
Records of divorce by Act of Parliament are held by the House of Lords Record Office (Parliamentary Archives). The records consist of the Act itself, and the written evidence

submitted (filed by date in a series known as Main Papers). The evidence submitted also contains, from 1798, an official copy of the previous proceedings in the church court. However, almost all the relevant facts were given in oral testimony and therefore published as part of the record of the business of the House of Lords in the *House of Lords Journal.* Copies of the *House of Lords Journals* are sometimes available in libraries, so you may not need to visit the Record Office. If you do decide to make a personal visit, please note that an appointment is required and that you will not be able to proceed without knowing the date of the entry in the *Lords Journal.* The *House of Lords Journal* is indexed.

Records of actions in church courts are held in diocesan record offices, which are generally but not always combined with local record offices. The records can be complex and difficult to use. For advice on their location, arrangement and contents, use Chapman, Owen and Tarver [**45**]. Sometimes a decree of separation from bed and board was enrolled amongst the Chancery records (now at The National Archives in record series C 78).

Appeals from ecclesiastical courts in matrimonial cases were made to the High Court of Delegates, 1532-1832 (the records include an unpublished index; there is also a rare but published index, *A Catalogue of Processes in the Registry of the High Court of Delegates,* for cases 1609-1823, see **45**) and to the Judicial Committee of the Privy council, 1833-1858. The records are held in The National Archives under letter codes DEL and PCAP; they are easy to find via the online catalogue as they are listed by the name of the case. For further information see Bevan [**45**].

[*See* also: **30**; **37**].

After 1858
Records of divorces 1858-1943 are held at The National Archives in record series J 77; they are subject to a 75 year closure. Annual name indexes are available in record series J 78. Further information, including advice on how to seek access to closed files, is given by Bevan (a) [**45**].

33. Inquests (infanticide and abortion)

Coroners' records are something of a specialist subject. Until the early eighteenth century they are mainly in The National Archives, thereafter they are more likely to be in the local record office (if they survive at all, and many do not). Modern inquest records are closed for 75 years and may still be in the custody of the coroner. However, where an illegal killing was suspected, copies of the relevant documentation was often forwarded to the assizes even if the killer was 'persons unknown'. Before making any attempt to trace original records you should check local newspapers whose accounts of the inquest may actually be far more informative than the coroner's papers [37]. Then if you still want to pursue the original inquest report, consult Gibson and Rogers, *Coroners' Records* [45]. Early coroners' records for a number of counties have been published, so check to see what is available for your area. If you want to get more deeply into the subject look out for the publications of R F Hunnisett who has edited coroners' records for Nottinghamshire, Sussex and Wiltshire. The introductory essays to his editions provide clear and useful explanations of the context of the records and of the procedures that created and kept them that are of relevance far beyond the boundaries of the counties concerned.

34. FamilySearch (International Genealogical Index)

If you do not know the parish of baptism or marriage, especially for the period before 1837, then the International Genealogical Index (IGI) is the place to start. This is a world-wide index of births/baptisms and marriages. Chronologically, coverage for the British Isles is from the beginnings of parish registers in the mid sixteenth century to roughly 1885. Entries for England and Wales are mainly from Anglican parish registers and from the non-parochial registers in The National Archives, and some areas, for example Cheshire, Northamptonshire and Somerset, are only thinly covered. The International Genealogical Index or IGI is now largely subsumed within the FamilySearch website [46]. Like all indexes it has its errors, but you do not have to rely on the index alone. Using FamilySearch will identify the microfilm of the original source which you can then check for yourself, either at the record office concerned or at an LDS family history centre.

The main drawback of the IGI for those researching illegitimate relatives is that it is very much geared to tracing genuine ancestors: those who lived into adulthood and had a chance to leave offspring. It does not aim to include illegitimate children who died in infancy.

35. Law reports

Do not confuse the formal Law Reports with journalistic accounts of legal proceedings in the ordinary press. Law Reports were compiled by lawyers for lawyers and pinpoint the legal issues raised by a particular case, so they are often quite technical and difficult for laymen to appreciate fully. However they do provide a useful amount of detail; they usually give the names of the parties concerned and always indicate the date of hearing and the court of trial. Cases concerning illegitimacy often did raise important legal issues – rights of parents to custody, entitlement to poor law, rights to citizenship and inheritance, rules governing how and when summonses and writs could be served – and so the Law Reports do contain a wealth of information about some illegitimate children. The Law Reports are published in a series known as the *English Reports* and should be available to you via large reference libraries and specialist legal libraries. Searching the published volumes is unwieldy and time consuming, but many of the drawbacks have been overcome by the free text search facility on the newly issued CD-ROM version. The CD-ROM *English Reports* is expensive and does not appear to be widely available in the UK outside specialist legal libraries, so you may need to seek advice from a librarian (or friendly lawyer) about how best to access it. A copy is available at The National Archives.

36. Manorial records

If your illegitimate ancestor or his/her parents were manorial tenants then it will also be worth looking at the records of the local manorial court. Such records are often scattered in a number of different archives, so you will probably need to consult the Manorial Documents Register to locate them. It is compiled and maintained by the Royal Commission on Historical Manuscripts (now part of The National Archives) who will respond to written enquiries. Parts of the register (Hampshire, Isle of Wight, Norfolk, Yorkshire and Wales) are available online via the Internet [**46**].

Only a small proportion of the records created before the sixteenth century still survive, but a number of early manorial court rolls have been published, so it is also worth seeking advice at a good central reference library or at the local studies library for the area concerned. A number of cases of bastardy are considered by Poos and Bonfield [**45**]. Like all formal legal documents manorial court records are in Latin until 1733. They were often written very hurriedly, so they can be extremely difficult to read; fortunately interpreting them is made easier by the use of a fairly standard format. For help on using manorial records see Ellis, Harvey, Park, Stuart and Travers [**45**].

37. Newspapers, pamphlets and magazines

Everyone wants to read about a good scandal. Our ancestors enjoyed them, too. Sex and violence have always been good selling points, so whether you are looking for scandal about your ancestors' adultery or parentage, reports of wife sales, inquests, criminal trials or salacious legal actions, always remember to check published sources.

Some of these, such as national newspapers and upper-class periodicals like the *Gentleman's Magazine*, are fairly general in their coverage. The *Gentleman's Magazine* is indexed, and so too is the London *Times*. The *Times* index is especially useful, not only because the newspaper has had a continuous existence since the mid 1780s, but because the index is published on CD-ROM and because the *Times* itself is widely available on microfilm in reference libraries throughout the UK. Local newspapers, as their name implies, restrict their coverage to specific geographical areas; provincial local papers date back well into the eighteenth century but local papers for the London area did not really take off until the late nineteenth century.

The national newspaper library is part of the British Library [47]. Copies of newspapers are also held in many other libraries and archives across the UK and there is a major initiative – Newsplan – to preserve them and to make them more widely available on microfilm. To locate them use Gibson, *Local newspapers* [45] or the various regional Newsplan sites [46]. Some of these sites indicate whether locally compiled indexes are available.

There were also publications that specialised in sensationalism. Do not fall into the common error of believing that the gutter press was invented in the late nineteenth century. From 1769 to 1790, the *Town and Country Magazine* reported the extra-marital affairs of the upper classes with considerable relish. In the early 1790s, the *Bon Ton Magazine* concentrated on society scandal and is a rich and extremely readable (but possibly not very reliable) source for precisely those juicy tidbits that more respectable newspapers did not care to report. Actions for adultery were reported in the press and in pamphlets from at least the early eighteenth century. It is clear that some of these accounts were written by the participants themselves in an attempt to appeal to public opinion, almost in the way that we might expect prominent individuals to target TV talk shows in our own day.

Trials, especially those resulting in the death penalty, also spawned their own literature in the form of pamphlets and dying speeches. Sometimes these developed into a series of works: trials at the Old Bailey in London, for example, have been regularly and reliably reported in a series of pamphlets of variable title (but now usually known as the *Old Bailey Sessions Proceedings*) since the late seventeenth century. Copies are now available online [46]. Similar series of pamphlets are available for a number of other courts: extracts from many of have been used in the microfilm publication *British Trials* [45]. Short accounts of the lives of notorious criminals also found a ready market and were sometimes collected together and re-issued in book form. Perhaps the best known of these collections is the *Newgate Calendar* which has been appeared in various forms from the early eighteenth century to the present day.

Finding (and buying) this kind of published material has been made much easier with the advent of electronic catalogues. The catalogues of the British Library and of the

Library of Congress are both available online over the internet and will enable you to conduct sophisticated preparatory searches. Their books, of course, are available only to personal visitors. Other specialist libraries, including subscription lending libraries such as the London Library, also have their catalogues on the web, as do many secondhand and antiquarian booksellers. The *English Short Title Catalogue* is a major international collaborative venture that aims to identify all printed works in English printed before 1800; it is available on CD-ROM in many major libraries. An earlier (and less ambitious) version of the project was known as the *Eighteenth Century Short Title Catalogue* and is also available on CD-ROM and in microform. Confusingly, both versions of the project are generally abbreviated to *ESTC* so if you need pre-eighteenth-century publications make sure you check which version you are using.

38. Police records

The records of the Metropolitan Police Force are held at The National Archives in record series that have the prefix MEPO. Material relating to investigations by the Metropolitan Police are mainly held in MEPO 2, MEPO 3 and MEPO 4 at The National Archives. There is also a surviving Metropolitan Police register of murders and deaths by violence that includes the deaths of women by illegal abortion for the period 1891-1909, 1912-1917 and 1919-1966 in MEPO 20.

The records of other police forces are held locally. They may be held by the police force itself or by a police museum rather than by the local record office. There is a good but now dated guide to police records by Bridgeman and Emsley [**45**] which will get you started. You might also find it useful to look at Sherman, *My Ancestor was a Policeman*. However you need to be aware that the survival of police records is generally poor and that incidents such as finding an abandoned child or the body of a baby or very small child, were so commonplace in the past that they rarely attracted the kind of attention that they would receive now.

39. Poor law records before 1834 (the 'old' poor law)

The pre-1834 system generated a wide range of records. Before 1801 some parishes (usually rural ones) made a point of taking written statements from all new residents renting property worth less than £10 so that they could establish the correct parish of settlement and possibly ask for a certificate long before any poor relief was required. These statements were known as 'settlement examinations'. Other parishes only took settlement examinations from those in need of relief. The settlement examination may, or may not, have led to a removal order (that is, an order to send the pauper back to his/her parish of settlement) or to the production of a certificate of settlement (a legally binding agreement in which the parish of settlement acknowledged responsibility for future poor relief for named individuals). It may also have been used in the course of negotiations with the parish of settlement and have led to correspondence, accounts, legal opinions and appeals.

In bastardy cases one could expect to find examinations, orders, bonds and warrants. Additional information may also exist in the parish accounts (constables', churchwardens', and overseers'), correspondence and even in vestry minutes. Some parishes had workhouses long before 1834, so their records should also be explored. If a single mother were receiving regular payments from the parish, or if a bastard were being fostered out, then it may also be worth checking lists of names of those described as the 'parish poor'. These were lists of those entitled to receive long term relief. They were sometimes written into the back of the audited accounts, sometimes written into registers and sometimes printed. The lists were essentially an anti-fraud measure and they were usually compiled annually.

Bastardy and other poor law material relating to a single individual can be found in a number of places. Bastardy examinations could be taken before a single justice of the peace but any resulting order had to be signed by two justices acting in petty sessions. The holding of petty sessions was not regulated until the early nineteenth century. Before that time they were held as and when convenient. They might cover a single parish, or a wider area. They might be held for a specific purpose such as the annual 'brewster' sessions for licensing public houses. Some areas were well served by petty sessions; others were not. In those areas that did not have regular petty sessions, where there were comparatively few active justices, or where the nearest petty sessions was too far away, it was often more convenient for the parish officers to get the alleged father bound over to appear at the quarter sessions. Sometimes the decision to bind a man over to quarter sessions rather than issue an adjudication at petty sessions seems to have been tactical and was probably designed to force him to acknowledge his responsibilities voluntarily. So even in undisputed cases there are three possible search strategies: the poor law and vestry papers of the parish of residence and of the alleged parish(es) of settlement (sometimes referred to as the 'parish chest'); surviving petty sessions minutes; quarter sessions files and papers.

If the case were disputed and there was a formal appeal then the records of the appeal are likely to be amongst those of quarter sessions. Some appeal cases were referred to the court of King's Bench; almost all these cases are reported fully in the formal Law Reports [35]. Surviving quarter sessions papers and local vestry papers are to be found in local record offices. Many local record offices, Family History Societies and individuals have indexes of settlement and bastardy papers. Use Gibson and Hampson,

Specialist Indexes to locate them [**45**]. If you find such an index make sure that you check exactly what it does – and does not – cover. It often transpires that the index is to records found amongst quarter sessions papers rather than amongst those of the parish. It will probably be necessary for you to check both types of collection. Settlement certificates, and perhaps other papers too, also survive in private hands.

For more information on using old poor law records see Cole, Herber and Tate; there are some good illustrations of the sort of documents created by bastardy cases on the Powys Digital History website [**46**]. You may also find it useful to consult the Wiltshire Family History Society's reprint of *The Compleat Parish Officer* which contains an abstract of the law as it applied in 1734, together with many examples of poor law documents [**45**].

40. Poor law after 1834 (the 'new' poor law)

As with the 'old' poor law, the administration of poor relief by Boards of Guardians after 1834 generated a wide range of records. They include minutes of meetings and sub-committees, correspondence, workhouse registers of admissions, discharges, religious affiliation (sometimes known as Creed Registers), births, baptisms and deaths, records of admissions/referrals to infirmaries and asylums, applications for out-relief, registers of pauper children admitted to poor law schools or those sent to attend schools run by other institutions, registers of children boarded out with foster parents and registers of children emigrating. The records may also include adoption agreements; some are known to survive from at least the 1860s. Any or all of these may assist your search; even formal minute books sometimes included details about individuals. It is most unlikely that there will be any indexes, or that there will be a complete set of records for any particular area.

Applications for affiliation (maintenance) orders 1834-1844 could only be made by the Poor Law Union. This gives you a double chance of finding information: in the poor law records and in the records of the quarter sessions who had to process the orders. Poor law records are worth searching even after 1844, since copies of affiliation orders had to be sent to the Guardians.

Boards of Guardians were abolished in 1930 when their responsibilities passed to County Councils. Similar records for the period after 1930 are therefore amongst the records of the County Council, usually the Welfare Department (often later renamed Social Services). These too are likely to be held in the local record office. Some poor law infirmaries later became National Health Service hospitals and their records have been subsumed into hospital records rather than those of the local authority. The

National Archives and the Wellcome Foundation have developed a database of hospital records (known as HOSPREC) which can be consulted on their premises, but which is also available online [46].

In order to locate poor law records, you will need to identify the poor law union responsible for your ancestor. Many local record offices have indexes to institutions and maps of poor law districts that will help for their own areas, but for a national overview and for the locations of records, you should use Gibson and Young *Poor Law Union Records;* there is a more detailed guide to records in the London area by Webb [45]. Although surviving records are held in local record offices, it is not always obvious which one, because some Poor Law Unions straddled county borders. Check before you visit!

The local records of Poor Law Guardians can also be supplemented by their correspondence with the central government. Copies of such correspondence are held at The National Archives, mainly in record series MH 12. These can be informative about individuals or about incidents, such as an unexplained death in the workhouse, that either required government advice or attracted government interest. However they are poorly listed, difficult to use and survival before about 1871 is sparse. Do not attempt to use them until you have exhausted local possibilities. For further advice on The National Archives holdings see Bevan [45].

41. Private papers

The term private papers covers a rag bag of possibilities, from the personal correspondence of wealthy families, to estate records, diaries (of ordinary people as well as the great and good), documents held by local solicitors, and family bibles. They could include strays from official records, such as quarter sessions, private adoption agreements, deeds of separation, gossipy letters, copies of maintenance agreements, or even, if you are amazingly lucky, the working papers of the doctor or midwife who delivered your ancestor. They may still be held in private hands, or may have been deposited on loan or as a gift in a local record office or specialist archive. They may also be subject to restricted access conditions. To locate them use Foster and Shepherd [45], or consult the databases at the National Register of Archives, or Access to Archives which are available online over the internet [46].

42. Rescue homes, mother and baby hostels, emigration schemes and adoption societies

Many mother and baby hostels, rescue homes and orphanages were of purely local importance and may have been short-lived. Some, like Dr Barnardo's, began as local institutions and then developed into national ones; others were administered by organisations, such as religious foundations, that already had a national presence. In order to locate their records you need to know the correct name of the institution; you may also need to identify what organisation was responsible for running the home or adoption society concerned. Use trade directories to do this, or if this fails seek advice of staff at the local studies library or local record office for the area concerned. Bear in mind the possibility that responsibility for the home (and its records) may have passed to another organisation in some kind of administrative re-shuffle: government departments and private businesses are not the only organisations that have had to face the challenge of merger and take-over. If it were a poor law institution then go back to **40**. The most complete guide to adoption records is Stafford [**45**], but you will probably also find it useful to consult Foster and Shepherd [**45**] or the online databases at the National Register of Archives or Access to Archives [**46**]. It may seem obvious that any surviving records should be held locally, but this is not necessarily so. The surviving records may be filed in several different series: the Salvation Army, for example, not only have (incomplete) returns from their mother and baby hostels but also sometimes have records of interviews with the mothers. Some adoption societies have very full files that include photographs, correspondence and details of next of kin. This kind of record may also be subject to stringent access conditions, especially for those less than 75 years old. Equally there may be nothing. You will not know until you try.

If you are researching a child who was sent abroad by a children's emigration scheme then you should also check what records are available in the country of adoption. The web pages of the National Archives of Canada contain a searchable database of 'Home Children' mentioned in incoming passenger lists (follow the links via ArchiviaNet); there is much useful information on the Young Immigrants to Canada site, which also includes information about Australia and Bermuda as well [**46**]. Coldrey's guide [**45**] is available online on the web pages of the National Archives of Australia [**46**]; these pages also contain useful advice about starting a search and a link to the Australian Directory of Archives. For Canada see also Horn [**45**]. You might also want to consider joining the Rootsweb e-mail group specifically for those researching British home children [**46**].

British passenger lists for ships going to Australia, Canada, New Zealand and South Africa between 1890 and 1960 are held at The National Archives in record series BT 27, but there are no name indexes and in order make a search feasible you will need at least two of the following three pieces of information: the date of departure; the name of the ship; the port of departure. For further information see Bevan [**45**].

Another possible angle on rescue homes is to trace their reports and newsletters. These may survive with the original archive of the society, but copies are likely to turn up in many other places, such as private papers of subscribers and officials as well as in libraries. Such publications can simply be rather dry accounts of the year's activities, but they often served a secondary purpose – to publicise the cause and to attract (and retain) subscribers. As a result, many contain case studies of children who were helped and may even include testimonials from some of the children themselves. Even if they do not they will help provide an insight into the children's lives by telling you about its facilities, its ethos, and the names of its subscribers. They may even tell you how much it cost to keep a child there and include pictures of the home and its grounds.

43. Trade directories

Trade directories have been produced for London since the late seventeenth century but they are sparse before the late eighteenth century; provincial directories generally date from the early nineteenth century. Most local studies libraries and record offices will probably have a collection of directories for their areas. The best national collection is held at the Guildhall Library in London, but you will not need to make a personal visit as it has been published on microfilm. Other excellent national collections are held at the library of the Society of Genealogists, and at the National Art Library (Victoria and Albert Museum). Published catalogues of these holdings are available [45]. It is also worth checking whether directories have been re-published in facsimile, micro-form or on CD-ROM.

44. Wills

Wills before 1858
Until January 1858, the probate of wills was a matter for the ecclesiastical (church) courts. The structure of the courts was quite complicated as it matched the hierarchy of the Church of England. The choice of a court of probate theoretically depended on the size and location of any real estate. However there were also other factors and in practice most executors probably had a choice of courts. They might choose the lowest possible court in order to avoid unnecessary expense. Conversely they might choose a higher court as a way of demonstrating their own superior social status.

Wills provide high quality evidence about your ancestor's life and world. They are a particularly useful source for tracing illegitimate children because of the link between legitimacy and inheritance rights. For a good overview of the laws and customs of will-making see Herber [45].

There is no single national index to wills proved before 1858 but indexes and transcripts have been published for a number of courts and these will obviously make your searches more manageable. From 1796 estate duty registers also give the court of probate and so act as a rough annual index in their own right. The registers for the period 1796-1857 are available on microfilm at The National Archives and LDS family history centres and online through TNA's Documents Online website. Registers for 1858-1903 are held at The National Archives; indexes are available. No registers survive after 1903. To find the most likely courts of probate for your person, together with a description of the surviving records and available indexes use Gibson, *Probate Jurisdictions* [**45**]. Copies of wills proved in the Prerogative Court of Canterbury (PCC) are available on microfilm at The National Archives (and online), as well as at LDS family history centres. Other PCC probate material, such as inventories and material relating to disputed wills, is produced only at The National Archives and is more fully described in Scott, and Bevan [**45**].

Wills after 1858

In 1858 the jurisdiction of the church courts over wills was abolished and a single court of probate was established instead. There are annual indexes to wills proved since that date. These are available for public consultation at the Probate Searchroom of the Principal Registry of the Family Division [**47**]. Microfiche copies of the indexes 1858-1943 are available at the Society of Genealogists, The National Archives and LDS family history centres and at a number of other libraries and archives. Some of the indexes are available online on the Ancestry.co.uk website. Copies of the wills can be ordered in person at the Probate Searchroom or at any District Probate Registry provided you know when and where the original grant of probate was issued. If you are unable to attend in person, you should make a postal application to the Court Service in York [**47**]. Files and papers relating to disputed probates after 1858 are at The National Archives in record series J 121, but only a 7% sample survives, see Bevan [**45**].

Intestacy

As indicated above [**2**], estates of single illegitimate persons who died intestate were technically forfeit to the crown. Correspondence about intestacy (and petitions asking the Crown to waive forfeiture) occasionally survives amongst the records of the Treasury; similarly some surviving papers relating to legal actions in respect of the estates of intestates are amongst the records of the Treasury Solicitor (both held at The National Archives). Where an illegitimate person died intestate whilst serving in the armed forces, it may also be worth extending your search out of the usual run of service records into the general administrative papers of the service concerned. These records are also held at The National Archives.

PART IV: FINDING YOUR WAY AROUND

45. Guides to records and research

A catalogue of processes in the registry of the High Court of Delegates, 1609-1823 (London, 1823).

Access to birth records: information for people adopted in England or Wales (Department of Health and Office for National Statistics).

The adoption contact register: information for people adopted in England or Wales and their birth relatives (Department of Health and Office for National Statistics)

Barrow, G B, *The genealogist's guide* (London and Chicago, 1977).

Bevan, A (ed.), *Tracing your ancestors in the Public Record Office,* (5th edn. PRO, 1999).

Bevan A, (a) *Divorce 1858 onwards* in *Ancestors* magazine, Oct/Nov 2002.

Bond, M F, *Guide to the records of Parliament* (HMSO, 1971).

Breed, G R, *My ancestors were baptists: how can I find out more about them?* (SoG, 1995).

Briant Rosier, M E, *Index to census registration districts* (FFHS, 1995).

Bridgeman, I and C Emsley, *A guide to the archives of the police forces of England and Wales* (Police History Society, 1989).

British Isles genealogical register or *BIG-R* (FFHS, several editions with indexes, 1994-1997).

British trials 1660-1900 (Chadwyck-Healey, 1990).

Caley, I S, *National genealogical directory* (annual, 1979-1993).

Chapman, C, S*in, sex and probate: ecclesiastical courts, officials and records* (2nd edn. Lochin, 1997).

Chapman, C, *Marriage laws, rites, records and customs* (Lochin, 1996).

Chapman, C, *Pre-1841 censuses and population listings* (4th edn. Lochin, 1994).

Clifford, D J H, *My ancestors were congregationalists in England and Wales* (2nd edn. SoG, 1997).

Coldrey, B, *Good British stock: child and youth migration to Australia, 1901-83* (National Archives of Australia, Research Guide 11).

Cole, A, *An introduction to poor law documents* (2nd edn. FFHS, 2000).

The compleat parish officer (1734 edn reprinted 1996, Wiltshire FHS).

Ellis, M, *Using manorial records* (PRO, 1994).

Foster, J and J Shepherd, *British archives: a guide to archive resources in the United Kingdom* (3rd edn. Macmillan, 1995).

Gerhold, D, *Courts of Equity – a guide to chancery and other legal records* (Pinhorn, 1994)

Gibson, J S W, *Bishops' transcripts and marriage licences: a guide to their location and indexes* (4th edn. FFHS, 1997).

Gibson, J S W, *Local Newspapers 1750-1920* (FFHS, 1989).

Gibson, J S W, *Probate jurisdictions* (4th edn. FFHS, 1997).

Gibson, J S W and M Medlycott, *Local census listings, 1522-1930: holdings in the British Isles* (3rd edn. FFHS, 1997).

Gibson, J S W and E Hampson, *Marriage and census indexes for family historians.*

Gibson, J S W and E Hampson, *Census returns on microform, a directory to local holdings* (6th edn. FFHS, 1994).

Gibson, J S W and E Hampson, *Specialist indexes for family historians* (2nd edn. FFHS, 2000)

Gibson, J S W and P Peskett, *Record offices: how to find them* (8th edn. FFHS, 1998)

Gibson, J S W and C D Rogers, *Coroners' records in England and Wales* (2nd edn. FFHS, 1997).

Gooder, E, *Latin for local history, an introduction* (2nd edn. Longman, 1984).

Harvey, P D A, *Manorial records* (BRA, 1984).

Hawkings, D T, *Criminal ancestors* (Sutton, 1992).

Herber, M D, *Ancestral trails*, (revised edn. Sutton, 2000).

Higgs, E, *A clearer sense of the census: the manuscript returns for England and Wales, 1801-1901* (PRO, 1996).

Horn, P, 'The emigration of pauper children to Canada, 1870-1914' in *Genealogists' Magazine,* XXV (SoG, June 1997).

Horwitz, H, *Chancery equity records and proceedings 1600-1800, a guide to documents in the Public Record Office* (revised edn. PRO, 1998*).*

Johnson, K A and M R Sainty, *Genealogical research directory* (Sydney, published annually since 1982).

Keen, M E, *A bibliography of trade directories of the British Isles in the National Art Library* (Victoria and Albert Museum, 1979).

Lawton, G, 'Using the Bernau Index' in *Family Tree Magazine* (VIII, 1991-2)

Leary, M, *My ancestors were methodists: how can I find out more about them?*(revised edn. SoG, 1999).

London directories from the Guildhall Library, 1677-1900 (EP Microform, 1995).

Lumas, S, *Making use of the census* (PRO, 1997).

Lushington's Law of affiliation and bastardy (London, many editions, mainly twentieth century).

McLaughlin, E, *Reading old handwriting* (2nd edn. McLaughlin, 1995).

McLaughlin, E, *Simple Latin for family historians* (5th edn. FFHS, 1994).

McLaughlin, E, *The censuses 1841-1881* (4th edn. FFHS, 1990).

Marshall, G W, *The genealogist's guide* (4th edn, 1903; reprinted London and Baltimore, 1967).

Maxted, I, *British national directories, 1781-1819* (Exeter, 1989).

Newington-Irving, N J N, *Directories and poll books ...in the library of the Society of Genealogists* (6th edn. SoG, 1995).

National index of parish registers (SoG, 1968-).

Norton, J E, *Guide to the national and provincial directories of England and Wales, excluding London, before 1856* (RHS, 1950).

Owen, D M, *Records of the established church in England* (BRA, 1970).

Paley, R, *Using criminal records* (PRO, 2001).

Park, P B, *My ancestors were manorial tenants: how can I find out more about them?* (2nd edn. SoG, 1994).

Poos, L R and L Bonfield, *Select cases in manorial courts 1250-1550* (Selden Society, 1998).

Raymond, S, *English genealogy, a bibliography* (3rd edn. FFHS, 1996).

Rogers, C D, *Tracing missing persons in England and Wales* (Manchester University Press, 1986).

Ruston, A, *My ancestors were English presbyterians/unitarians: how can I find out more about them?* (SoG, 1993).

Saunders, T W, *The law and practice of orders of affiliation and proceedings in bastardy* (London, many editions, c1844-1900).

Scott, M, *Prerogative Court of Canterbury wills and other probate records* (PRO, 1997).

Sharp, H, *How to use the Bernau index* (2nd edn. SoG, 2000).

Shaw, G and A Tipper, *British directories: a bibliography and guide to directories published in England and Wales (1850-1950) and Scotland (1773-1950)* (Leicester University Press, 1988).

Sherman, A, *My ancestor was a policeman* (SoG, 2000).

Shorney, D, *Protestant non-conformity and Roman Catholicism: a guide to sources in the Public Record Office* (PRO, 1996).

Simpson, E, *Latin word list for family historians* (FFHS, 1985).

Stafford, G, *Where to find adoption records a guide for counsellors* (London British Agencies for Adoption & Fostering, 1985).

Stuart, D, *Latin for local and family historians* (Phillimore, 1995).

Stuart, D, *Manorial records* (Phillimore, 1992).

Tarver, A, *Church Court Records: an introduction for family and local historians* (Phillimore, 1995).

Tate, W E, *The parish chest: a study of the records of parochial administration in England* (3rd edn. Phillimore, 1985).

Thomson, T R, *Catalogue of British family histories* (3rd edn., London 1980).

Travers, A, 'Manorial Documents' in *Genealogists' Magazine,* XXI (1983), pp 1-10.

Trowles, T, 'Eighteenth century exchequer records as a genealogical source' in *Genealogists Magazine,* XXV: 93-8.

Watts, C T and M J, 'In the High Court of Justice …' in the *Genealogists' Magazine,* XX:200-206.

Webb, C, *London, Middlesex and Surrey Workhouse Records* (West Surrey FHS, 1991).

Whitmore, J B, *A genealogical guide* (London 1953), parts 1-4.

Wiggins, R, *Registration districts* (2nd edn. SoG, 1998).

46. A select list of useful websites

Name	Website address
1841-1911 census	www.nationalarchives.gov.uk/records/ census-records.htm
Access to Archives	www.a2a.pro.gov.uk
AIM 25	www.aim25.ac.uk
British Library	www.bl.uk
British Library Online Newspaper Archive	www.uk.olivesoftware.com
Cyndi's List (includes adoption-related pages)	www.cyndislist.com
Equity Pleadings Database	www.records.pro.gov.uk/equity/person_srch.asp
Familia	www.familia.org.uk
FamilySearch	www.familysearch.org
Federation of Family History Societies	www.ffhs.org.uk
Guild of One-Name Studies	www.one-name.org/
GENUKI	www.genuki.org.uk/
General Register Office England and Wales	http://www.gro.gov.uk/gro/content/ certificates/
HOSPREC	www.hospitalrecords.pro.gov.uk
Institute of Historical Research	www.history.ac.uk
LDS	www.familysearch.org
Library of Congress	http://catalog.loc.gov
London Library	www.londonlibrary.co.uk
The National Archives (formerly the Public Record Office)	www.nationalarchives.gov.uk
National Archives of Australia	www.naa.gov.au
National Archives of Canada	www.archives.ca
National Archives of New Zealand	www.archives.govt.nz/welcome.html
National Register of Archives	*see* The National Archives
Newsplan - London and the South-East	www.newsplan.co.uk/
- Yorkshire and the Humber	www.yli.org.uk/newsplan
- Devon	www.devon.gov.uk/library/locstudy/ newsplan.html
Old Bailey trials 1674-1834	http://oldbaileyonline.org
Palaeography courses online	www.english.cam.ac.uk/ceres/ehoc http://paleo.anglo-norman.org/palindex.html
Penance	www.le.ac.uk/elh/pot/research/penance.html
Powys Digital History Project	http://history.powys.org.uk/history/intro/ entry.html
Probate	www.courtservice.gov.uk/cms/3724.htm
Public Record Office	*see* The National Archives
Rootsweb Genealogical Data Co-operative	www.rootsweb.com
Royal Commission on Historical Manuscripts	*see* The National Archives
Royal Historical Society Bibliography	www.rhs.ac.uk/bibwel.asp

Name	Website address
Society of Genealogists	www.sog.org.uk
Workhouses	www.workhouses.org.uk
Young Immigrants to Canada	www.ist.uwaterloo.ca/~marj/genealogy/ homeadd.html

47. Useful addresses

Name	Address
British Library	Main site: 96 Euston Road, London NW1 2DB Newspaper Library, Colindale Avenue, London NW9 5HE
Federation of Family History Societies	PO Box 8857, Lutterworth, LE17 9BJ
Guild of One-Name Studies	Box G, 14 Charterhouse Buildings, Goswell Road, London EC1M 7BA
Guildhall Library and Manuscripts	Aldermanbury, London EC2P 2EJ
London Metropolitan Archives	40 Northampton Road, London EC1R 0HB
Manorial Documents Register	*see* The National Archives
The National Archives (formerly the Public Record Office)	Kew, Richmond, Surrey TW9 4DU
National Archives of Australia	PO Box 7425, Canberra Mail Centre, ACT 2610, Australia
National Archives of Canada	395 Wellington Street, Ottawa, Ontario K1A 0N3, Canada
National Register of Archives	*see* Royal Commission on Historical Manuscripts
General Register Office Certificate enquiries	PO Box 2, Southport, Merseyside, PR8 2D
Parliamentary Archives	House of Lords, London SW1A 0PW
Probate (after 1858):	
London searchroom	First Avenue House, 42-49 High Holborn, London WC1V 6NP
Postal applications	The Postal Searches and Copies Dept., York Probate Sub-Registry, Duncombe Place, York YO1 7EA.
Royal Commission on Historical Manuscripts	*see* The National Archives
Society of Genealogists	14 Charterhouse Buildings, Goswell Road, London EC1M 7BA
Wellcome Library for the History and Understanding of Medicine	Wellcome Building (2nd floor), 183 Euston Road, London NW1 2BE

APPENDIX 1: Glossary of synonyms for bastardy

This glossary is based largely on the work of Dr R J Hetherington. For full details of the published sources used by Hetherington see his article 'Synonyms for bastards' in *Birmingham and Midland Society for Genealogy and Heraldry Journal*, no 36 (Feb 1975).

Adulterine
Adulterous
Anonymous
Bantling (from banc 'bench')
Bar sinister
Base, base-born
Bast (packsaddle – used by muleteers as a bed.)
Bastard (born on a bast)
Basturtly gullion (a bastard's bastard – Lancashire dialect)
Bastardus
Begotten in adultery/fornication/incest
Born by chance
Born extra
Born in bastardy
Born of adultery
Born out of wedlock
By-blow
By-chop
By-scape
By-slip
Chance bairn
Chance begot
Chance born
Chance child
Chance come
Chanceling
Child of shame
Come by chance
Ex fornicatione nata (born in fornication)
Father unknown
Filius adulterinus (child of an adulterer)
Filius fornicatoris (child of a fornicator)
Filius meretricis (child of a harlot)
Filius naturalis
Filius nescio cujus (child of one unknown)
Filius nullius (no one's child)
Filius populi (child of the people)
Filius scorti (child of a harlot)
Filius terrae (child of the country)
Filius unius cujusque (child of everyone)
Filius vulgi (child of the multitude)
Fruit of adultery

Illegitimate, illegitimus
Impure natus (impure birth)
Incerti patris (true father uncertain)
Incestuous child (incestuous may be used as a synonym for lack of chastity but it can also refer to the forbidden degrees)
In concubinatu nati (born in concubinage)
In sin begotten
Lanebegot (NB Although this word is often cited in family history publications, Hetherington identifies it as a mistranscription of 'lovebegot')
Left-handed children
Lovebegot
Lovechild
Manser (child of harlot)
Merrybegot
Misbegotten
Nameless
Natural son
Nothus
Offspring of adultery
One of the children of the people
Prolea spuria (spurious issue)
Puer populi (child of the people)
Reputed child of [named individual]
Scape-begotten child
Son of adultery
Son of a gun (conceived near the gun on a man-of-war and logged as 'son of a gun')
Son of a harlot
Son of no certain man
Son of the people
Son of shame
Spuriosus, spurius
Stupriproles (offspring of 'stuprum' incest or shame)
Supposed son (also supposititious, suppositus, supputed)
Unlawfully begotten
Viciatus (from 'vicium' a fault)
Whoreson
Without a father
Without a name

APPENDIX 2: A simplified research plan

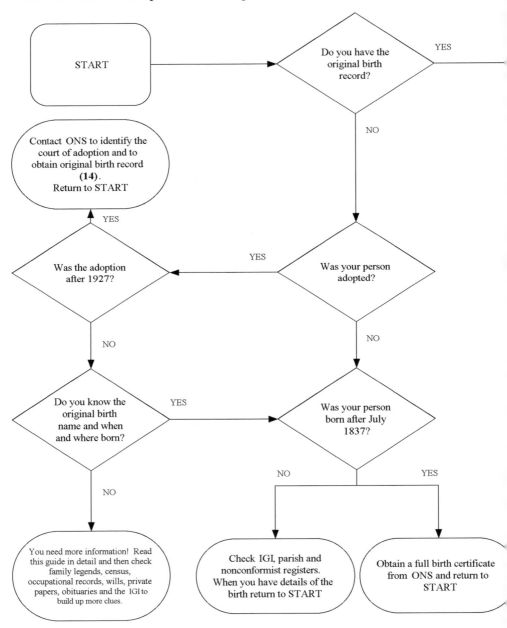

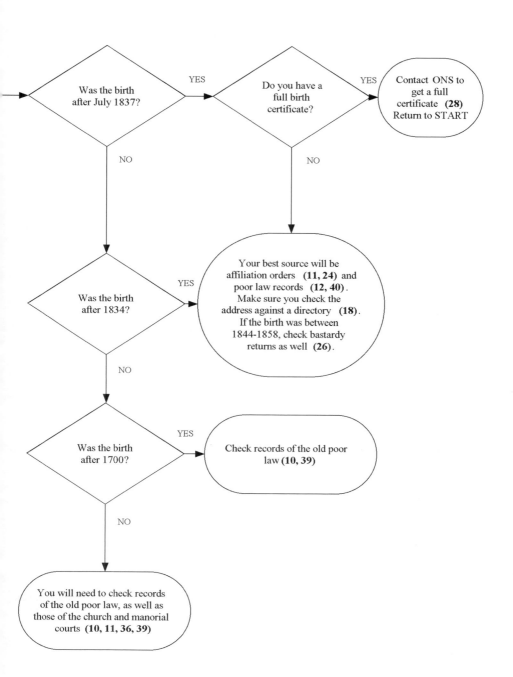

Was the birth after July 1837?

YES

Do you have a full birth certificate?

YES

Contact ONS to get a full certificate **(28)** Return to START

NO

NO

Was the birth after 1834?

YES

Your best source will be affiliation orders **(11, 24)** and poor law records **(12, 40)**. Make sure you check the address against a directory **(18)**. If the birth was between 1844-1858, check bastardy returns as well **(26)**.

NO

Was the birth after 1700?

YES

Check records of the old poor law **(10, 39)**

NO

You will need to check records of the old poor law, as well as those of the church and manorial courts **(10, 11, 36, 39)**

INDEX

SOCIETY OF GENEALOGISTS
The National Library & Education Centre for Family History

Other SoG titles...

MY ANCESTORS WERE

GYPSIES

SHARON SILLERS FLOATE

A guide to Gypsy sources for family historians
Third edition

£8.99

MY ANCESTOR WAS...

IN SERVICE

PAMELA HORN

A guide to sources for family historians

£8.50

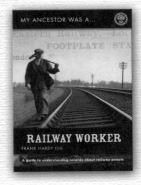

MY ANCESTOR WAS A...

RAILWAY WORKER

FRANK HARDY FSG

A guide to understanding records about railway people

£7.50

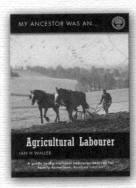

MY ANCESTOR WAS AN...

Agricultural Labourer

IAN H WALLER

A guide to Agricultural Labourer sources for
family historians. Revised edition

£8.99

MY ANCESTOR WAS A...

COALMINER

DAVID TONKS

A guide to coalminer sources for family historians.
Second edition

£9.50

How to get the most from
Family Pictures

BY JAYNE SHRIMPTON

£12.99

Order online at: **www.sog.org.uk** or call: 020 7702 5483.
Also available from the Society's bookshop.

14 Charterhouse Buildings, Goswell Road, London EC1M 7BA
Tel: 020 7251 8799 | Fax: 020 7250 1800 | **www.sog.org.uk**

Registered Charity No. 233701. Company limited by guarantee. Registered No. 115703.
Registered office, 14 Charterhouse Buildings, London, EC1M 7BA. Registered in England & Wales